Click Here!
— for a well-trained dog —

by Deborah A. Jones Ph.D.

Illustrated by Susan L. Coons

Click Here! for a well-trained dog

by Deborah A. Jones Ph.D.

©2002 Deborah A. Jones
ISBN 1-888994-19-3

Published by: Howln Moon Press
203 State Road, Eliot, ME 03903
207-439-3508
Printed and bound in the United States

Designed by: Howln Moon Press
Illustrations: Susan L. Coons
Photographs: courtesy of the author

Library of Congress Cataloging-in-Publication Data

Jones, Deborah A.
   Click Here! for a well-trained dog / by Deborah A. Jones Ph.D.
      p. cm.
   ISBN 1-888994-19-3 (alk. paper)

— Table of Contents —

Acknowledgments

Sharing a joyful moment with Copper.
— *photo courtesy of the Author*

everything that I do. Also, thanks to Kathy Ginther for reading and proofing early drafts of the manuscript.

I would like to thank and acknowledge all of the trainers and owners out there who have inspired me and supported me by their desire to find and use kinder and gentler training methods. Thanks in particular to the community of Association of Pet Dog Trainer (APDT) colleagues who have so generously shared ideas and provided unwavering support.

My appreciation goes to my wonderful publisher, Betty Mueller, for her support and encouragement in this and in all my writing projects. She has made it very easy for me to become a published author! And also thanks to Susan Coons, the very talented illustrator, who gives this book its wonderful look.

Finally, thanks to all the great dogs who have been my true teachers. They have shown me, quite clearly, what works and what doesn't! Thanks to my wonderful 'once in a lifetime' dog, *Katie* the Labrador Retriever, (U-CD Katherine Tempy Micajah CDX, TT, CGC, Delta Society Pet Partner) the one who started it all; to *Sully* the Golden Retriever (Sullivan's No Fool CD), who keeps me humble and makes me always try new techniques; and to *Copper* the Papillon (U-CDX Dewdrop's I'mtoosexyformyears CDX, AX, AXJ, CGC, NAC, NJC, NGC, CL3-R, CL2S), who makes it all look so easy.

There are many, many people who have helped me to complete the writing of this book. First, thanks to my business partner, Liz Mancz. Liz not only provided excellent editing and proofreading, but she also took up the slack at our business, Planet Canine, to allow me time to work on the book. Thanks also to my mother, Ruth Rice, for her proofreading and comments, and for her unwavering support in

Introduction

This dog training book presents a technique commonly known as clicker training. Clicker training may be very different from the methods you've heard of or used before. While the difference alone may be intriguing, that's not enough. Clicker training is also better. It's faster, more effective, more humane, and more fun (for both you and your dog).

As a responsible pet owner, you've probably looked through a number of books, trying to find the one that makes the most sense and seems the most useful. I know, because I've been through them all myself. There's an enormous amount of information available, yet much of it isn't exactly what you're looking for. Some of the books are too old or dated, some are too complicated, some are too simple, some seem too harsh, some just don't work. Finding a good dog training book can be confusing and frustrating.

It helps to ask yourself a few questions when trying to evaluate dog training information.

First, what are the author's credentials? Is the author an experienced trainer? How much experience and what kind? Does the author have any advanced academic degrees in animal behavior or psychology?

Second, does the method make sense? Can you understand why it works? Is the author able to provide clear and simple explanations for the underlying theory?

Third, does the method seem fair and kind? What's your 'gut' feeling about the method? Would you be comfortable using the techniques?

Fourth, do you think you can actually succeed using the method? If it relies on special skills and abilities, you might have trouble making it work. Also, will the method work with most (if not all) dogs, or only with a certain type of dog?

If you evaluate dog training information using this type of critical thinking and questioning, you should be able to make an educated, informed decision.

Our pets are vitally important to us. For many of us, they are more than just animals, they are our families. We enjoy their company and find comfort in their presence. Dogs can add an important emotional and social dimension to our lives. However, in order to be good lifelong companions, these family members need proper care, socialization, and training.

The purpose of this book is to provide you with information on clicker training. Over the years, I have found clicker training to be the absolute best method available. Not only does clicker training result in a well-behaved dog, it will also strengthen your bond and relationship. The clicker provides a clear and strong communication channel between you and your pet. Once that communication is established, you will see amazing changes in your dog's behavior and in your relationship with your dog.

*Our pets are vitally important to us. We enjoy their
company and find comfort in their presence.*

Chapter 1

Dog Training for the New Millennium

— Amazing Changes —

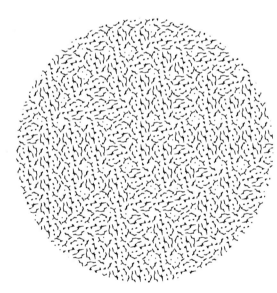

I. Dolphins, Chickens, Wolves and Sheepdogs

Clicker training is one of the newest, yet one of the oldest, animal training methods. Sound confusing? Actually, both statements are true. While many trainers are just starting to learn about clicker training, it is based on scientific learning principles (operant and classical conditioning theories) that have always existed.

Animal trainers are beginning to see the effectiveness and usefulness of clicker training methods. Many experienced dog trainers are just now learning about clicker methods, having tried many different techniques over the years. Marine mammal trainers are way ahead of dog trainers. They learned, early in the evolution of their field, that the scientific principles underlying clicker methods were the most effective way to train. While they often use whistles instead of clickers, the rest of the techniques are identical.

Clearly, marine mammal training and pet dog training pose different, unique challenges. It would be silly to say that dolphin training and dog training are exactly the same. Dolphins live in tanks of water, dogs live in our homes with us. The physical structure of the two species is very different. They eat different types of foods and they play in different ways. So what can dog trainers and owners possibly learn from dolphin and marine mammal trainers?

Actually, there are many commonalities. All creatures learn in the same way; through experience. No matter what the species, experiences alter behavior. When a dolphin jumps out of the water and gets a fish for his efforts, learning has occurred and he is likely to repeat the action in the future. When a dog jumps up on the counter and finds a bologna sandwich, learning has occurred and he is likely to repeat the action in the future. The most basic learning principle applies in both cases. Consequences determine whether or not behavior will be repeated, whether you're dealing with a dolphin, a dog, or a chicken.

• *KEY CONCEPT: Consequences determine whether or not behavior will be repeated.*

In fact, chicken training camps and workshops have become very popular among dog trainers. Bob Bailey (a marine mammal trainer) and Marion Breland Bailey (a psychologist and student of the famous B.F. Skinner — who is considered the founder of operant conditioning) have designed and held chicken training camps for the past few years. Because the principles of learning are the same, regardless of species, chicken training can be a great way to practice clicker techniques. In some ways chickens are harder to train than dogs. First, a chicken doesn't form a close social bond with a human, as many dogs do. Second, chickens tend to move very quickly, making it hard to 'catch' the behavior that you like. Third, chickens can be downright nasty! Of course, some dogs can be too. However, if you can train a chicken, you've learned quite a bit about how to train a dog.

My chicken training experience was quite humbling. As I already had quite a bit of dog training experience, I thought it would be simple. Was I ever wrong! I fumbled the chicken feed and missed many of my chances to click. Within a couple of training sessions, I became convinced that my chicken hated me. I was frustrated that I wasn't making quick progress. I felt just like a novice, which was great for reminding me how hard this can seem to new trainers.

Clicker training seems new to many dog owners because it is very different from old-fashioned approaches. Many traditional, commonly-known dog training methods rely on the use of physical force and/or coercion to gain compliance. These methods often came out of military and police canine training. While these training styles may have seemed appropriate for certain types of dogs who were bred and trained for particularly difficult or dangerous tasks, they now seem unnecessarily harsh and rough. And just try to force a chicken to behave in any particular way! You'll get squawked at and pecked, but you probably won't get much compliance.

Many of our ideas on canine behavior and training are derived from theories and observations based on wolf pack interactions. This information, while sometimes useful, may also be misleading. Ethologists often study wolves living in the wild or in sanctuaries that approximate natural conditions as closely as possible. They examine the relationships between pack members and make conclusions based on those observations. This information has helped us to understand more about wolf behavior and relationships. Because the wolf is the dog's closest wild relative, many scientists, trainers, and owners have applied theories on wolf behavior to domestic dogs.

While it might seem logical to apply findings about wolves to dogs, it could lead to mistaken assumptions. The conditions in which dogs and wolves live are very, very different. Most wolves are born in the wild and are not exposed to humans during their early development. Wolves have to provide for their own shelter and sustenance. Wolves breed freely, without human interference. Dogs, on the other hand, are often tended by humans from the moment of conception. They are provided with food, water, and shelter. Their breeding is controlled by surgical means and through strict management (usually). These differences, plus many, many others, make direct comparisons between wolf and dog behavior problematic.

DOGS ARE NOT WOLVES!

Observers of wolf behavior have documented relationships within packs. In packs, they can identify the alpha male and female (the two highest ranking wolves and often the only ones who breed), and then a hierarchy of ranking into which the other wolves are ordered down to the omega (lowest pack member). It has been observed that higher ranking wolves enjoy certain privileges such

as having first access to important resources. Higher ranking wolves are also responsible for protecting the pack from harm and providing leadership. It has been suggested that humans should interact with their pet dogs in the same ways that wolves interact with each other. This has led many pet trainers and owners to have some strange ideas about attaining and maintaining control within their 'pack'; mainly through physical force and intimidation. Methods that force dogs into submissive postures have been advocated, even though these methods can often make problems worse, rather than better. In the wild, wolves communicate through very subtle body language and signals, and their interactions rarely escalate to physical confrontations.

Many trainers have suggested that we should treat our pet dogs as an alpha dog would. This may seem like a reasonable suggestion, but it has one major flaw. We are not dogs, and our dogs realize that. Also, we are not very good at being alpha dogs. True alphas are very subtle in their body language and interactions with the pack. Most humans are not.

YOUR DOG KNOWS THAT YOU'RE NOT ANOTHER DOG, SO DON'T TRY TO ACT LIKE ONE!

The idea of 'dominance' has been a popular one among dog owners and trainers. The leader or alpha is considered to be dominant and is in charge of the pack. It has been suggested that many behavior problems in dogs occur because the dog is trying to be the dominant pack member. Some of the behavior problems that have been blamed on dominance include barking, jumping, growling, biting, stealing food, guarding objects, ignoring owners, and destructiveness. While the concept of dominance may have some value in limited cases, it has definitely been overused.

There are many possible causes for problem behaviors. Approaching every interaction with your dog with the "dominance-as-cause" mindset can be counterproductive. Thinking in terms of dominance sets you up in a competitive situation with your dog. It suggests that one must win and the other lose. Many people think that in order to be dominant, you must force your dog to be submissive. This confrontational approach can be damaging to your relationship with your dog. With clicker training, you will be building a cooperative, rather than a confrontational, relationship. Instead of competing with your dog for the 'top spot' through force and physical means, you will be a fair and humane leader through your understanding of canine behavior and your use of learning principles.

Our relationships with our dogs have evolved over time. In the past in the United States (as well as in many other parts of the world) dogs were often treated as livestock, rather than as family members. Dogs who performed jobs such as hunting, guarding, or herding were kept and used, but not necessarily integrated into life within the household. As with other working animals, dogs were typically dirty, smelly, and full of parasites. They were kept outside in dog houses, kennels, or barns.

They were exposed to many physical dangers and often not immunized against common diseases. Working and farm dogs often were killed in accidents. It would be emotionally painful to become overly attached to a working dog, who would probably not live a full lifespan.

This is not to say that people didn't feel affection for their animals, but it was probably not as intense as it is for those of us who live with our dogs in very close proximity. In the past, usually only the very rich could afford to keep 'house dogs' for companionship purposes only. Today, many pet owners have dogs strictly for social and emotional reasons, not for practical ones. Dogs have become our friends and our family. They give us a feeling of connection and emotional support. Most of us have a mental image of Lassie, the perfect dog who symbolizes devotion, intelligence, and protection. Lassie is often portrayed as much smarter than her humans. We don't expect much from our canine friends, do we?!

Unfortunately, that stereotypic image of the perfect dog can cause problems. If you're reading this book, your dog probably isn't acting quite like Lassie. Now, rationally, you know that Lassie is not a real dog, but a myth. However, particularly if you grew up with that canine image of perfection (as I did), on some emotional level you might be at least slightly disappointed when your dog doesn't approach that image.

In fact, your dog may seem to be the total opposite of your expectations, and that can be very frustrating and disappointing.

II. What Are Dogs?

So far in this chapter I've been telling you what dogs are not. Dogs are not dolphins, they are not wolves, and they are not Lassie. So, what are they?

Considering how closely people live with dogs, we understand very little about them. However, in order to devise the best training methods possible, it helps to know why dogs behave the way they do and what motivates them.

I am constantly amazed by the misconceptions that people still have about dogs. In particular, many people believe that dogs have human thought processes and emotions. While some dogs are indeed very intelligent, their thought processes are not nearly as complex as those of people. Dogs are capable of understanding some basic relationships between events, but they do not have higher level reasoning abilities.

• *KEY CONCEPT: Dogs don't think like humans.*

Dogs seem to operate on a level similar to what's known as the sensorimotor stage of cognitive development in people. The sensorimotor stage lasts for about the first two years of a child's life. In this stage, a child experiences and understands the world primarily through the physical senses and by actual experience manipulating objects. In human infants, the senses of touch and taste are primary. That's why babies need to touch

Dogs have a much larger part of the brain devoted to scent than do humans.

everything and love to put objects in their mouths. It's their way of learning about the world.

In dogs, we know that smell is a primary sense, followed by taste and vision. Take a dog into a new environment and he'll explore it by sniffing. Dogs have a much larger part of the brain devoted to scent than do humans. Show a dog an unusual object and he'll sniff it, then he may try to eat it, especially if he's a retriever! This behavior shows that dogs perceive the world in a very different way than humans. Show a human an unusual object and he'll examine it visually, then touch and manipulate the object. We need to keep this perceptual difference in mind when we start considering the reasons for canine behavior. For example, most dogs sniff each other on meeting. This is their way of identifying each other through scent, rather than through sight. When a dog sniffs a human we label this behavior as 'rude'.

However, the dog is simply learning more about the person; It's a 'getting to know you' behavior.

Certain breeds have been selected for their ability to follow a scent trail. A friend of mine has a Black and Tan Coonhound. When we traveled together I was amazed at how much Tarra used her nose. In a new hotel room she went over every single piece of furniture, sniffing every inch. Tarra probably learned an amazing amount about all the former occupants of the room, including whether they were male or female, what they ate, and what kind of soap or cologne they used. She might as well have been blind for all she used her eyes, yet she gleaned more information from her senses than I did.

Because dogs have sensations and perceptions that are very different from those of humans, we shouldn't be surprised that they process information in very different ways than us. Dogs seem to be oriented in the present. It's not that they don't display the ability to remember, It's just that current circumstances seem to override everything else. Also, while dogs do display a basic understanding of specific associations (a principle which we use in clicker training), they are not capable of sophisticated cause and effect logic.

Hardly a day goes by that a client doesn't tell me "My dog knows that what he did was wrong." Most people don't stop to think that concepts of right and wrong are subjective human ideas. For example, we believe that it's wrong for the dog to go to the bathroom in the house. Granted, it's not a good idea, as our houses would become disgusting very quickly. However, young puppies (and young humans!) with no previous training have absolutely no clue that it's a problem to go wherever they happen to be when the urge hits. To them, going in the house is no different than going anywhere else. It's only wrong because it is something that we don't want them to do.

So what makes people become so sure that "the dog knows he was wrong"? Actually, this conclusion is based on an incomplete understanding of canine body language and communication signals. Imagine this scene: you walk into a room to find a large puddle and your puppy. You take a deep breath and tense all your muscles, probably thinking "not again!" Your puppy, being very good at reading subtle body language, immediately picks up on your signals that something is wrong. He might not be sure exactly what, but it is clear to him that you are upset. In response, he displays submissive and appeasing body language.

This display might include any of the following: lowering himself to the ground, creeping, possibly going belly up, putting his ears back, looking away, licking his lips, and (in extreme cases) submissively urinating. These signs are all canine ways of saying "calm down, don't be upset". However, most people misread these as signs of guilt, an emotion that dogs aren't capable of having. To feel guilt you have to be able to understand right from wrong, and we have absolutely no evidence that dogs think that way.

Many of my clients had dogs as kids and now have a dog for the first time as an adult. They think that because they are familiar with dogs, they understand them. For many of us, dogs are part of our nostalgic childhood memories. The family dog was perfect as far as we can recall. We remember romping in the yard, a dog lying quietly at our feet, maybe even teaching Fido how to shake hands. What we don't remember are the barking, the housetraining accidents, and the massive shedding problems. In fact, we may not have even been aware of the problems. I tell clients to ask their parents about the family dog, mom and dad are much more likely to have a realistic view rather than an idealized one. When we take that idealized view into a relationship with a new dog, things will probably not go as expected. The new dog can't possibly live up to our expectations. They are, after all, real living and breathing creatures, not fuzzy pleasant memories.

III. Choosing the Right Dog for You

Dogs are different things to different people. Each dog is a unique individual. One of their biggest attractions is that they seem to fill whatever roles we need them to fill. Dogs come in many varieties with radically different physical forms, behavioral tendencies, and personalities. That means that the perfect dog for everyone is out there! Unfortunately, many people make very poor choices. They choose dogs who do not fit their needs. Sedentary apartment dwellers may choose a very active dog like an Australian Shepherd, then be upset when the dog becomes bored and destroys the furniture. Families with young children may choose a small, fragile dog like a Papillon, then be upset when the dog gets hurt and becomes fearful and snappy towards children. A very active person who wants a jogging companion may choose a Newfoundland, then be unhappy that the dog is too large and slow to accompany him on his runs. By analyzing your lifestyle and needs, you can choose an appropriate and compatible pet.

If you want to care for and nurture another living creature, and would like a dog who will cuddle on the couch, you can find a dog who would be happy to fill that role. I call my Golden Retriever, Sully, a 'love sponge'. He would be very happy to lie next to you for hours while you fuss over him. However, other Golden Retrievers might be bouncing off the walls without more activity. If you want an active dog to accompany you while you go hiking, biking, and swimming, there are many dogs who would absolutely adore that lifestyle.

In fact, many dogs need this level of physical activity and don't get it regularly. If you want a dog to make you feel safe and secure, the typical Labrador Retriever who loves everyone may not be the right dog for you. However, there are many breeds with a more protective and cautious nature. You do have to be very careful though, that such a dog is extremely well-bred, well-trained, and well-socialized.

Those protective tendencies can easily develop into aggression.

I've owned purebred as well as mixed breed dogs. There are advantages and disadvantages to choosing either. With a purebred you can have a good idea of size, coat type, possible inherited physical disorders, and basic personality traits. For example, you could make an educated guess that a Wire Fox Terrier puppy will remain relatively small, have a short curly coat, be very active, be vocal, and possibly have a tendency to dig (as many terriers do). If you have specific needs, a purebred dog is a bit more predictable. However, mixed breed dogs can be absolutely wonderful pets and companions. Be aware that eventual size and behavior may be harder to gauge than with purebreds. One advantage to acquiring a mixed breed is that you are often taking a dog from a shelter or humane society and giving it a chance at a good life. There are so many mixed breeds out there that most shelters are overwhelmed, so you are doing a VERY GOOD THING by adopting an unwanted dog.

One way to combine the advantages of purebred and mixed breed dogs is to adopt an older dog from a purebred rescue. Rescue organizations take unwanted dogs of a particular breed, keep them in foster homes or facilities, and adopt them out to pet owners. Most rescue dogs are adults who have lost their homes for a number of possible reasons that may have nothing to do with the dog's personality and behavior (owner's death, divorce, moving, financial difficulties, etc.)

The best dog I have ever owned is my Labrador Retriever, Katie, who I got as an 18-month-old from a rescue organization. Older dogs can bond closely to you and they can be well-behaved with proper handling and training. In fact, clicker training is especially well-suited to older dogs and adopted dogs who may need to learn new/better behaviors.

Many people choose a puppy rather than an adult dog. Puppies are definitely appealing. They have the same types of features that draw us to human children. Both have big eyes, high foreheads, small mouths, and a rounded body shape. Both make cute little noises and smell good (usually!) In addition, most puppies are cuddly and fuzzy. While we find ourselves attracted to puppies, a puppy may not be the best choice for everyone. On the down side, puppies need almost constant monitoring and care, have needle-like teeth that they love to use, tend to be very active, can be quite destructive, and have no house manners. It's important to be realistic when first acquiring a puppy. I can almost guarantee that there will be frustrations and disappointments, no matter how much you wanted the pup or how well-prepared you try to be. When your puppy screams every hour on the hour for five nights in a row, it's hard to remember exactly why you ever wanted him. However, if you understand the potential difficulties and have educated yourself in ways to deal with them you won't be so upset when they inevitably occur.

Something that many pet owners fail to consider are the likely breed and behavioral tendencies of any particular dog. This is probably the biggest mistake that people make in choosing a dog. Often, people choose a dog based on looks and size, and don't consider personality factors. When choosing a specific breed, do some research first. Find out what the breed was originally designed to do. For example, herding dogs, such as Border Collies and Shelties, have inborn behavioral tendencies that include circling, barking, and possibly nipping at heels. These tendencies are necessary to perform herding, but not so great when they're directed towards humans. However, if you know that these are likely behaviors, you can start early to work on decreasing them, or finding an appropriate outlet for them.

The typical, and very sound advice that you not choose an extremely cautious or an extremely pushy dog or puppy is good. Unfortunately, many times people aren't aware of personality problems until it is too late. We tend to get caught up in how cute and appealing a puppy is, and we're not very critical consumers. Once you fall in love with a puppy, your good sense often goes right out the window! If at all possible, get an experienced trainer to help you choose an appropriate pet. You need an evaluation from someone who can be objective, and not overlook potential behavior problems.

If you are looking for a purebred dog, it is important to find a reputable breeder. You can call the American Kennel Club to ask for a list of breeder referrals. However, it's vital that you ask the breeders the right questions.

Once you fall in love with a puppy, your good sense often goes right out the window!

You want a breeder who has done the appropriate health checks for the parents. It's best to buy a puppy whose parents have earned their conformation championships. This assures you that the breeder has a genuine knowledge and understanding of the breed. You should ask to see the parents, or at least the mother. Much of a dog's basic temperament (personality tendencies) is genetic, so you can learn a lot by seeing the puppy's relatives. A good breeder will interview you and ask plenty of questions about your lifestyle and your experience with dogs. If the breeder is only concerned about whether your check will clear the bank, keep looking.

You should NOT obtain a puppy from a pet store or a newspaper advertisement. Most pet stores buy their stock from puppy mills (despite what they say). Puppy mills are horrible places that mass produce animals with little regard to health and quality of life. Many puppies from pet stores are genetically unsound both physically and psychologically. Typically, they are also overpriced.

With a newspaper advertisement, you never know what you might get. Many people simply decide to make some money by obtaining a couple of purebred dogs and breeding them. These are called backyard breeders. Often, they have no understanding of the breed, its specific needs, and possible health problems. This type of breeder may be uneducated concerning proper early puppy care, dog training and behavior in general, and often will not be aware of the possible health and temperament problems with their specific breed. They are usually unwilling to provide health guarantees and ongoing advice and assistance on your puppy's needs and care.

Remember that you're making a long-term commitment when buying a dog. Most dogs average a lifespan of fifteen years. As my business partner Liz often says "if I wanted to be in a bad long-term relationship, I would have married someone from my high school."

Most people spend more time deciding on a car than on a puppy. Take your time and do your research. The right dog can enhance your life in many ways. The wrong dog can bring lots of heartache and grief.

IV. Crossover Dogs & Trainers

So what if you already have a dog that's not perfect? You are probably reading training books because you would like for your dog to be better behaved. The good news is that all dogs can be taught to behave in ways that you desire. Clicker training is a very effective, humane, and gentle way to make these changes. Even if you've used other methods or techniques in the past, it's never too late to change over to clicker training.

The term 'crossover' comes from a clicker trainer named Corally Burmaster. This term can refer to dogs who have been trained with other methods or to owners/trainers who have been using other training methods, and have decided to cross over to clicker training. The other methods are usually more forceful and punishment-based (as has been common among pet owners and trainers).

Change is difficult. Many pet owners, however, are motivated to find a better way (meaning a more effective and gentle one) to train their pets, and are willing to change their methods and techniques. Change actually needs to occur on several levels. There needs to be an internal change, a new perspective on dogs and their training, as well as the external change, learning new methods and techniques. Making these changes can take some time and effort, but the results are definitely worthwhile.

The internal changes that are required when you cross over to clicker training are probably more difficult than the external ones. In order to truly understand the philosophy underlying clicker training and to use clicker training most effectively you need to change your perspective on dogs, their behavior, how they learn, and how best to teach them. You are actually changing your basic assumptions about dogs, or what psychologists call your paradigm. The term paradigm refers to your perspective or the way you view the world. Your paradigm contains your understanding of how things are and how you expect them to be. The first step in changing your paradigm is to admit that your current one might be inaccurate or flawed. If you cannot admit the possibility of being wrong, then you cannot change and you are trapped in your current paradigm. However, if you can open up enough to consider alternate viewpoints and conflicting information, then you have the chance of being able to alter your perspective.

Some of your basic assumptions about dogs and their training may have to change if you are truly ready to move to clicker methods. Some of these misconceptions include the following ideas:

Assumption Number One: *Punishment is the best way to teach dogs what not to do.*

This is a common misconception. Those who understand clicker training know that this is not correct. Punishment has many possible side effects and can actually interfere with the learning process. Also, it is much more effective to teach dogs the appropriate behaviors (what we do want) instead.

Assumption Number Two: *Dogs do things out of spite (like chewing the couch cushions because you left them alone).*

First, the idea of being spiteful or getting even seems to be a uniquely human one. Second, dogs act in certain ways because the consequences are enjoyable, so they must find cushion chewing a pleasant experience. There's no need to consider more complex reasons for behavior.

Assumption Number Three: *A dog who does not obey you is showing a lack of respect for you.*

There are many possible reasons that a dog might not obey. For example, maybe he doesn't really understand what you're asking. Or maybe there is something too distracting happening at the same time. Plus, the idea of respect ties back into the dominance or alpha concept, and can be problematic for your relationship with your dog if overused. Even if you know, intellectually, that the assumptions listed above aren't true, on an emotional level people retain and act upon them. They can remain, even though buried, and pop up now and again. It helps to know that these old assumptions are there and that they are likely to be resistant to change.

Crossover dogs have their own challenges when the owner/trainer begins clicker training. When you change your entire approach to training, it may be confusing for your dog at first. Dogs who have been trained by more traditional methods have often learned that it's safest to do nothing. We have taught them not to try new things, because they might get punished. Ironically, dogs who are the most highly trained through old-fashioned methods are the least likely to open up and offer new behaviors. Old-fashioned training methods squelch attempts at active learning.

Clicker training encourages your dog to be an active participant in the learning process. This activity includes trying out new things (in a training session) until he hits on the right one. It may take some time for your dog to understand that new behaviors are now being encouraged and rewarded, rather than discouraged and punished. In clicker training we want our dogs to be our partners in training; not to be forced into it. Karen Pryor (*Don't Shoot the Dog*) introduced the idea that training is something you should do WITH your dog, not something you do TO your dog. Clicker trained dogs display an enjoyment and enthusiasm for learning and training that you don't see when force-based techniques are used.

Many times owners seek out clicker trainers when other methods have failed. A dog may not have responded well to more traditional training, and has possibly been labeled as 'stubborn' or 'stupid' or 'spiteful'. Often trainers blame a lack of success on the dog rather than on the method (or on the trainer's lack of skill). This is unfair and often very damaging to the dog and owner. Many dogs react poorly to training that is confusing and/or forceful. They may simply shut down and not respond. This shutting down can be misinterpreted as stubborness by those who are not good at understanding canine body language. These types of dogs can blossom with clicker training. Once the expectations become clear and consistent, and training begins to make sense, dogs who used to shut down will start to shine.

Many dog behavior problems are made worse, rather than better, by traditional, force-based training techniques. Punishing behaviors like separation anxiety, whining, barking and especially aggression will often lead to an escalation of those problems. Problem behaviors that are caused by stress and anxiety are not likely to be cured by adding more stress and anxiety through punishment. When first crossing over to clicker training some people find it difficult to think in terms of attending to and rewarding the positive rather than attending to and punishing the negative. Actually, we often make the same mistake when dealing with children. Undesirable behaviors are quickly noticed and dealt with. Appropriate and desirable behaviors, however, are ignored. A child who is running through the house screaming is quickly attended to; while a child who is quietly playing with his blocks is ignored. This is the exact opposite of what we should be doing. Any kind of attention (positive or negative) is rewarding and whatever behavior we pay attention to increases. This is a really important point to remember. Attend to the behaviors you want to increase. Find ways to prevent or avoid the behaviors you want to decrease.

• KEY CONCEPT: *The behaviors you pay attention to will increase.*

V. Modern Dog Training

I've talked a bit about old-fashioned dog training and why it isn't optimal for learning. Modern dog training focuses on using brain power rather than muscle to control our pets.

Most dog owners don't want to hurt or frighten their pets in order to train them. If a gentle, yet effective method were available, people would use it. I find that my clients are thrilled when I tell them that we don't use force, choke chains, or pinch collars in our training. People are looking for a better way, they just need to learn how to do it.

Clicker training offers the alternative that people have been looking for. It's gentle, there's no force involved. Once you understand some basic principles of learning and a few clicker training guidelines this method can be very effective. Also, clicker training is fun, both for the trainer and for the dog. Your dog will absolutely adore the time he spends working with you, and will display a high level of enthusiasm and excitement for training.

For me, one of the most important aspects of clicker training is that it is based on respect for your dog. Clicker training allows your dog to maintain his dignity while changing his behavior. You form a working partnership with your pet rather than one based on force and intimidation.

If these ideas about training appeal to you, it's time to get started and become a clicker trainer!

KEY CONCEPTS REVISITED:

• *Consequences determine whether or not behavior will be repeated. This is the central principle of operant conditioning. By changing the immediate consequences, you can alter behavior. Clicker training is based on this simple idea.*

• *Dogs don't think like humans. Canine and human thought processes are very different. We are being unfair to our pets when we expect them to have human thoughts and emotions. These false assumptions lead us to have unreasonable expectations of our dogs.*

• *The behaviors you pay attention to will increase. Be aware that attention is the most powerful reward there is. Attention (positive or negative) is very likely to increase the behavior it follows. Pay attention to the behaviors you want to increase.*

For further reading:
The Lost History of the Canine Race *by Mary Elizabeth Thurston*
The Culture Clash *by Jean Donaldson*

Modern dog training focuses on using brain power
rather than muscle to control our pets.

Click!

Chapter 2

That Special Sound

— Music to Your Dog's Ears —

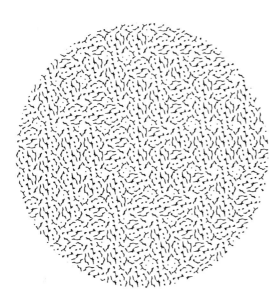

I. Slobbering Dogs & Television Commercials (classical conditioning)

This section will give you some background on how clicker training was discovered and developed. It will also provide you with some insight into how pervasive the use of learning theories is in our everyday lives.

Ivan Pavlov discovered that dogs could learn environmental signals very quickly. Pavlov was studying salivation in dogs (sounds exciting, huh?!) but ended up discovering a learning theory known as classical or respondent conditioning.

Pavlov was interested in the digestive process. His lab was set up to collect and measure the amount of saliva that dogs produced when they were presented with food. This is a natural connection in most animals — seeing or smelling food leads to salivation. However, he found that many dogs were salivating even when no food was present. When he started to investigate this phenomena he discovered that certain environmental factors could lead to salivation. These included hearing the banging sound of the metal food pans and seeing the lab assistant who usually fed the dogs. It even included people entering through the same door through which the assistant brought the food.

It seemed that the dogs had started to make connections between certain factors in the environment (the scientific term is stimuli) and receiving food. In anticipation of receiving food, the dogs would begin to drool. This connection, or association of events, is the basis of classical conditioning. The dogs learned that certain environmental stimuli signalled the presentation of food, and they began to react as if the food were already present.

• KEY CONCEPT: *Classical conditioning refers to learned associations between stimuli in the environment and an automatic reaction.*

The results of classical conditioning are present all around us. Have you ever seen a television commercial and suddenly become very hungry for the product, even when you had no desire for it before? Advertisers are counting on this. Just by seeing the product on television, your body can start to anticipate actually consuming the food, your gastric juices start to flow, and you become hungry.

People who smoke often report that certain situations trigger the desire for a cigarette. For example, sitting down with a cup of coffee has often been paired with smoking. When you try to stop smoking, that cup of coffee signals you that a cigarette should be coming soon, and your body starts to react accordingly.

My Labrador Retriever, Katie, has a classically conditioned response to bank drive-thru windows. Whenever I would go to a certain bank drive-thru, they would send a dog biscuit through for Katie along with my transaction. After a few connections, Katie began to anticipate the treat as we pulled up to the bank, and would begin drooling on my leg.

Katie had learned to associate the bank with food.

Many pets have learned to associate the sound of the refrigerator opening with receiving food. Even when you try to be very quiet, they will often rush to the refrigerator when it is opened. This will only occur if you have actually given the dog food from the refrigerator. If you have never given food from the refrigerator, its opening will have no meaning to the dog (classical conditioning has not occurred) and he will not react.

Imagine that you are walking down the street and you see a $100 bill lying on the sidewalk. You will most likely have an automatic and immediate emotional reaction to your good fortune. Your reaction to this find is based on your classical conditioning. If you have learned that money is associated with many other pleasant things, then you will be very excited. The paper and ink itself is not valuable, it is what the money has been connected with that is important. If a two-year-old child found the money, he would not have yet made the association, and would not understand the connection between the bill and other desirable objects.

When we teach our dogs to associate the sound of the clicker with positive events (things the dog wants and finds pleasant), we are using classical conditioning. This process, often called clicker conditioning, allows us to use the clicker as a training and communication tool. We will need to associate the sound of the clicker with things that our dogs find desirable. Once the basic connection has been established, then we can use the clicker in our training.

II. What is a Clicker?

Many of you might remember playing with small toys known as tin crickets when you were children. You could make the cricket click by squeezing it. In fact, they came in many different shapes and designs. The clickers that dog trainers use operate on the same principle, but they are designed to be sturdier and longer lasting. Or was I the only one who always broke my cricket within 5 minutes?

A clicker is a noisemaking device. The clicker is typically a small plastic box that easily fits in your hand. It has a metal mechanism inside. When you depress one end of the metal it makes a clicking sound. We use this sound as a signal to our dogs. It is a way to communicate with them. We teach our dogs that hearing the click is a very good sound.

The click will come to mean two things to our dogs. First, it is a behavioral marker, it tells the dog that he was doing something desirable at the very moment he heard the click. Second, it is a signal that a reinforcer (reward) will be forthcoming. Once the clicker becomes both a marker and a signal to your dog, it can be a very useful and effective communication tool.

• KEY CONCEPT: *The sound of the click becomes a marker and a signal to your dog.*

Your dog will come to love the sound of the clicker. In fact, he will start trying to figure out what you want and find ways to get you to click.

III. Building a Bridge

Marine mammal trainers use the term 'bridge' to refer to a behavioral marker. Their bridge is usually a whistle, as this is easy for dolphins to hear. The bridge is used at the exact moment that the desirable behavior is performed, and it is followed by a reinforcer (something that the animal will work to obtain). The marker bridges the timespan between the desired behavior and the presentation of the reinforcer.

The use of a bridge allows for a slight time delay between the desired behavior and the reinforcer. Sometimes it would be impossible to deliver the reinforcer itself at the exact moment we want to mark. For example, if a dolphin makes a particularly high jump, the trainer can whistle at the highest point in the arc, then the dolphin will finish the jump and come to the trainer for his goodies, possibly a bucket of fish. There is no way to actually deliver the fish while the dolphin is in the act of jumping. If you don't use a whistle to mark the behavior but wait until the dolphin lands after the jump and give him a fish then, you're rewarding him for being in the water, not for jumping. Without a bridge to provide information about the exact behavior being reinforced, the animal is left to think that whatever he was doing at the time he got the food is what you are rewarding and what you want him to repeat.

Imagine that you want to teach your dog to cover his eyes with his paw (hide your eyes). When he is beginning to try to perform this behavior, lifting his paw to his face, you want to mark that moment with a click. If you simply present a treat when he lifts his paw, he will not be clear about which behavior is being rewarded, as he must drop his paw in order to take the treat. Using a bridge makes it clear that lifting the paw is the desired behavior, not dropping it.

For dog training, we typically use a clicker as a bridge. The clicker will become a very special and important sound to your dog. The sound of the click induces a positive emotional state because it prepares your dog for a pleasant consequence (reinforcer). Another term (the scientific term) that is often used instead of bridge is secondary or conditioned reinforcer. This refers to the fact that the clicker (or whistle) is a learned marker that is connected to natural reinforcers like food or play (called primary reinforcers).

IV. Why Use a Clicker?

This question (why use a clicker?) is commonly asked by both pet owners and dog trainers.

At first glance, people are a bit skeptical that such a simple little device can actually be effective in training. It doesn't seem possible that a plastic noisemaker can be used to teach a dog anything at all. However, the clicker has many properties that make it a very useful dog training tool.

First, the clicker is a novel stimulus for most dogs. They have never heard anything like it before. This is ideal, because then we can use classical conditioning to associate the clicker with positive things like food and toys. Other types of sound are often heard in the environment (car horns, telephones ringing, beepers, etc.) and wouldn't be good training signals because they're so common and because they are meaningless to the dog.

Second, the sound of the click is clear and easily heard. Voices can get lost in the background noise. Also, many dogs have learned to ignore human voices; they're like Muzak (elevator music). They go on and on but don't really have any particular meaning to the dog. Even if you think your dog hangs on your every word, he probably simply picks up changes in tone or volume (and a few key terms like "dinner!") and ignores the rest.

Third, the click is fast. You can click faster than you can speak. Once you have practiced using the clicker it becomes almost automatic. This speed is important because you are attempting to click at the exact moment that your dog performs a desirable behavior.

Fourth, the click is consistent. It sounds the

same every single time. There are no variations in emotion or tone. Different clickers do have slightly different sounds; some are softer, some are sharper. However, those differences don't convey differences in the trainer's feelings or mood, as your voice might.

Some people are very suspicious about the claim that clicker training is fast, easy and effective. Those who have trained or attempted to train dogs in the past are the ones who are usually the most skeptical. Clicker training seems so different from the old-fashioned methods that it is hard to understand how and why it works. Also, clicker training principles oppose some very common and closely held beliefs about dog behavior and learning. For example....

1. Clicker training is hands-off. Many traditional methods require lots of physical handling on the part of the trainer, including the use of leash 'pops' and physically moving dogs into positions. It can seem as if you gain quick compliance using hands-on methods, but you are actually interfering with the active learning process.

2. Clicker training allows the dog to determine the rate of progress. Rather than setting arbitrary goals, clicker trainers learn to 'read' their dogs and adjust their training to the needs of the dog. This leads to fewer training failures and faster overall progress.

3. Clicker training allows the dog to make free behavioral choices. Many owners and trainers are consumed with the idea of control.

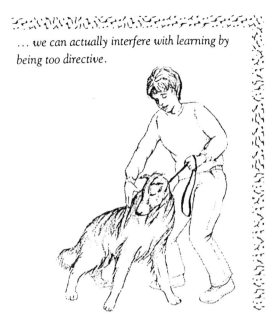

... we can actually interfere with learning by being too directive.

They are afraid to let the dogs make any movement without being directly in charge. While we obviously need to be able to exert control over our dogs' behavior, we can actually interfere with learning by being too directive.

4. Clicker training is not based on common dominance models of relationships between humans and dogs. These models are so pervasive in our interactions with dogs that it is hard to imagine that they might not be useful and correct. Clicker training is based strictly on scientifically tested learning theories, not on unproven ideas and assumptions regarding human-canine relationships.

5. Clicker training focuses on using positive training methods rather than on punishment-based ones. Many people truly believe that you cannot train an animal without the use of punishment. They believe that you must let the animal know when he is wrong and motivate him to avoid being wrong in the future by applying something unpleasant. Clicker trainers know that punishment can interfere both with learning and your relationship with your dog.

V. Who is a Clicker Trainer?

Clicker training has recently evolved as one of the newest types of dog training. It is still in its infancy in the field. Because of this, many trainers are not yet knowledgeable about its techniques and methods. They may simply be uneducated, or they may be applying clicker training ineffectively. Unfortunately, this can lead people to conclude that clicker training does not work. Instead of blaming a lack of understanding for training failures, the method itself gets blamed. This is unfair, yet not uncommon. An incomplete or erroneous understanding of the method doesn't mean that the method will not work if applied properly.

Dog trainers, even more than pet owners, may feel threatened by the introduction of a radically new training method. It will require trainers to rethink their approach to dog training and to learn new methods and techniques. This can be difficult, particularly for those who have many years of experience with other methods. As a pet dog owner looking for a clicker trainer, it is important to keep this in mind. There are good and bad trainers out there, and it is up to you to choose one that you are comfortable working with.

The newest buzz words in dog training are 'positive motivation'. When questioned, almost everyone who trains dogs will say that they use motivational methods. These words have become so overused that they are fairly meaningless. To use positive motivation can mean many possible things. It could mean the use of food, play, toys, praise, etc. However, it could also mean a mixture of methods, sometimes using 'goodies' and other times using force or punishment.

While some trainers are very good at making this sound like a reasonable approach, beware. There are a couple of fundamental flaws in this type of thinking. First, it can be very confusing for the dog. With clicker training we spend quite a bit of time and effort convincing our dogs to trust us. If we suddenly become forceful and frightening, our dogs will probably shut down and stop working. If we display inconsistent expectations and behaviors we are being unfair to our dogs. Second, dogs trained using the clicker are encouraged to be creative during training sessions and to offer behaviors (more on this later). Dogs trained using traditional methods are discouraged from doing anything other than what they are explicitly commanded to do. Trying to blend both of these techniques is doomed to failure.

There is a huge difference between using a clicker in training and being a clicker trainer. Adding the use of a clicker to other methods is a typical way to start. However, most people find that it is much more effective to go to a totally clicker-based technique. Someone who has truly become a clicker trainer has embraced the underlying philosophy as well as the basic training techniques. A true clicker trainer is dedicated to developing positively-based training methods and solutions to behavior problems. It takes a 'leap of faith' to move away from well-learned punishment-based methods and to explore more positive alternatives.

• KEY CONCEPT: *Using a clicker in training and being a clicker trainer are two very different things.*

When you are looking for a clicker trainer you need to do some research and ask some questions. You can start by calling area kennels, groomers, and veterinarians and asking them for referrals to trainers.

1. Call the trainers and ask them to describe their training techniques. Don't settle for very vague and general descriptions. Insist on specific explanations. Ask how the trainer would teach a puppy to lie down.

2. Ask for any written materials they have describing their methods. Also, ask the trainers which books they would recommend for pet owners.

3. Ask if you can observe a class without your dog. If the answer is "no", keep looking. When you observe, watch how the instructor interacts with both the owners and their dogs. Is the instruction clear and understandable?

What is the feeling or tone of the class? Do the methods seem successful? Does the trainer take time with each dog and handler?

4. Ask about the trainer's experience and background. However, keep in mind that quite a few years of experience is meaningless if the methods used are ineffective and/or inhumane. Degrees in psychology or animal behavior are an excellent background, but may not carry over into direct application to dog training. Earning titles in obedience competitions and/or agility trials is impressive, but doesn't necessarily indicate the ability to teach others.

5. Ask for references from past clients and call them. Obviously, the trainer will give you references of clients that he or she thinks were happy. You should ask the references specific questions such as "Are you still happy with the training you received from XYZ?" "Would you return to this trainer with another dog?" "What did you like best/least about the training you received?" "Did your dog seem to enjoy the training?"

It can be quite beneficial to find a good clicker trainer to help you get started. While it is certainly possible to train your dog using books and videos as your guides, hands-on help is always useful. Plus, if you are dealing with behavior problems, a clicker trainer or behaviorist might be a requirement.

KEY CONCEPTS REVISITED:

• *Classical conditioning refers to learned associations between stimuli in the environment and an automatic reaction. Classical conditioning occurs often in our daily lives without our awareness. For example, the sound of screeching brakes causes a startle reaction that leads us to get out of the street for safety. We use classical conditioning in clicker training to teach our dogs the initial connection between the sound of the click and the presentation of good things (primary reinforcers).*

• *The sound of the click becomes a marker and a signal to your dog. Once we have completed initial clicker conditioning (pairing the sound with good things) we can use the clicker to precisely mark those behaviors that we would like our dogs to repeat. The clicker also becomes a signal that the dog is going to receive a pleasant positive reinforcer. Dogs love to hear the clicker!*

• *Using a clicker in training and being a clicker trainer are two very different things. Many trainers have added the clicker to their training toolbox. They use it in addition to more traditional techniques. A true clicker trainer avoids the use of force and coercion and relies primarily on the use of positive reinforcement in training. Clicker training relies on a positive approach and philosophy that underlies the specific training techniques.*

Call the trainers and ask them to describe their training techniques.

For further reading:
Don't Shoot the Dog *by Karen Pryor*
Excel-erated Learning *by Pamela Reid, Ph.D.*

Chapter 3

Controlling the Goodies

— Becoming Master of the Canine Universe —

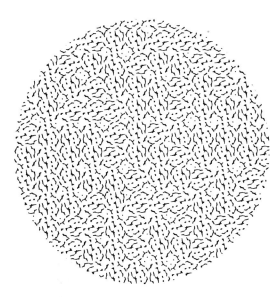

Human beings control almost all the things that dogs want. We have opposable thumbs and dogs don't. Therefore, we can work can openers. We can prepare food. We can throw tennis balls. We can open the door to the back-yard. We have the ability to access many things that our dogs would like to have.

We also have larger brains (melon brains rather than lemon brains according to Jean Donaldson) than our dogs. We have the ability to plan, to reason, and to deliberate. We can think about our dogs' behavior problems and plan ways to change them. We can consider possible outcomes to different training approaches. We can analyze the contexts in which undesirable behaviors occur. We ARE smarter than our dogs (most of the time)!

Simply put, we control the environment. Because of this, we can exert an enormous amount of influence over our dogs' behavior.

I. Primary Reinforcers — My Favorite Things!

What does your dog want? The things that you list in answer to this question are primary reinforcers. While dogs are individuals with specific likes and dislikes, as a species they have some preferences in common.

A primary reinforcer is defined as anything (object or activity) that your subject (regardless of species) has a need or desire for, and will work to obtain. Before you can start clicker training, you need to find out what primary reinforcers are available for you to use.

The correct scientific definition of a reinforcer states that it is anything that will increase the likelihood of the behavior that it follows. A positive reinforcer is a pleasant consequence that increases the probability of the preceding behavior. For example, imagine that you set your hamburger on the kitchen counter while you leave the room to answer the phone. Your dog smells the hamburger, jumps up on the counter, and eats it. His behavior, jumping up on the counter, was reinforced by finding and eating your hamburger. You now have a dog who is more likely to jump up on counters in the future. Your dog has learned from experience that counter surfing is a rewarding activity. We'll talk later about how to change this type of behavior once it is learned.

• KEY CONCEPT: *A reinforcer is anything that will increase the likelihood of the behavior that it follows.*

FOOD

The most common primary reinforcer for almost all species is food. Food is necessary to maintain life, but it is also very enjoyable to consume. Food has some wonderful advantages as a primary reinforcer. First, it is nearly universally desired and will work well for most dogs. Second, there are a wide variety of possible food reinforcers available, so you can usually find quite a few that will work for any particular dog. Third, the motivation for food is nearly constant, so it works as a

reinforcer most of the time. It can be quickly consumed after each presentation, then you can continue your training.

Some owners and trainers are resistant to the idea of using food in training. Common reasons given are:

"Fifi is very picky." and "Fifi has a delicate stomach."

Both of these reasons are usually mistaken assumptions. First, it is possible to teach a dog to become a picky eater by offering better and better tasting foods whenever she refuses what you have offered. Fifi learns that if she holds out and turns up her little nose, something much better will come along soon. Even better, Fifi may end up getting hand-fed and pampered.

Also, many dogs who are free-fed (have food constantly available) do not each much at any one time. Just imagine if you had a tasty buffet always ready on your kitchen counter. You'd probably eat small amounts throughout the day and never really feel hungry. However, if the food was only available at specified times you would eat a larger amount with more enthusiasm during those times.

"My dog is not allowed to have 'people' food because I don't want him to beg."

Dogs don't learn to beg because they are given 'people' foods during training sessions. They learn to beg because they are fed from your plate or from the table while you are eating.

If you never, ever feed your dog in those situations, your dog will not beg at those times.

"I WILL NOT bribe my dog with food!" and "I want my dog to work for me, not for food."

The first sentence suggests an incomplete understanding of the process of reinforcement. The reinforcer comes AFTER the desired behavior, and serves to increase the likelihood of that behavior. Bribes are given in advance of a behavior in the (usually false) hopes of making it more likely to occur. A bribe and a reinforcer are two very different things.

The second sentence suggests that the person has an incomplete understanding of canine learning and behavior. For most dogs, there is no advantage to performing a behavior that is not reinforced in some way. Dogs may act to avoid punishment or correction, or they may act to gain reinforcement. No matter what you might like to believe, they simply don't act just because they love you. Also, since much of what we ask them to do must seem completely irrational to them, we need to give them a good reason (pleasant consequence) to do things for us.

Properly used, food can be an incredibly useful reinforcer. For best results the food used should be small, soft, and very desirable. In general, use the smallest amounts of food that your dog will work for. This will probably vary with the size of the dog, but even some very large dogs will work for tiny crumbs. I use a treat the size of 1/4 of a Cheerio for my 8 pound Papillon, and the size of 1/2 of a Cheerio for my 65 pound Golden Retriever.

Occasionally, you may want to use a larger amount of a reinforcer in order to mark a particularly wonderful behavior or breakthough. This is called a jackpot. A jackpot can be very effective in marking a 'special' training moment. You can give a number of individual food reinforcers, one after the other. Or, you can give a large amount all at once, dropping a handful of treats on the floor for your dog or allowing him to eat the treats right out of the bag. A jackpot makes a major impression on your dog. He will remember the behavior that led to the jackpot.

A softer food works well because it doesn't require much time for chewing and swallowing. Foods like cheese, hot dog pieces, and soft cat treats are easy to swallow. They are also easy to divide into very small pieces.

A strong-smelling food, such as liver, works because the smell is so attractive to dogs that it gets and keeps their attention. Dogs are more scent oriented than visually oriented, so they are likely to notice and focus on interesting smells.

All food treats are not created equal. Plain, dry kibble may work fine in your living room but not in your front yard. Dull, boring treats will not motivate your dog to work for them, especially when there are more interesting things going on in the environment (other dogs, squirrels, children, etc.) A high-value, highly desirable treat should be used in more distracting situations.

It can also help to keep a variety of different food reinforcers available, rather than using the same ones day after day. Predictability leads to boredom. Your dog may be thinking "Yawn, another piece of hot dog, ho hum." To counteract this, we often use 'doggie trail mix'. The trail mix is simply a mixture of whatever food reinforcers are available at any given time. With each handful, there may be a different mixture. This keeps your dog's interest and enthusiasm high. For example, trail mix may contain garlic coated Cheerios, small pieces of microwaved hot dogs, tiny bits of string cheese, soft cat food treats, and bits of puppy kibble.

The truth is that someone else's reinforcers are always better than yours. In classes, we often trade reinforcers and find that our dogs love what's new and different.

Some favorite food reinforcers you can make at home:

Garlic-coated Cheerios. Empty the Cheerios into a large bowl. Add a generous portion of garlic powder (NOT garlic salt) and mix. You can add some parmesan cheese for extra flavor as well. If you return the Cheerios to the original box be sure to mark them as garlic-flavored. One client of mine had a son who poured a big bowl, added milk and sugar, and got a nasty surprise with the first bite!

Microwaved hot dogs. You can use any kind of hot dogs for this. I prefer the low-fat variety.

Cut each hot dog lengthwise into 4 strips. Then chop the strips into tiny pieces. Place the chopped hot dog pieces on a microwave safe plate. Cover with a paper towel. Cook on high for 5-7 minutes, depending on your oven. The hot dog pieces should be dried out and almost crispy. These treats will keep indefinitely.

NOTE: Mixing the garlic-flavored Cheerios and the microwaved hot dogs together results in a wonderful tasting reinforcer as the flavors blend well. At least, the dogs think they do!

Baby food brownies. You can make doggie brownies with a few simple ingredients. The basic recipe can be altered by adding or changing ingredients. For example, you can use real pureed liver rather than the baby food. You can substitute oatmeal for the cornmeal. You can also add garlic and parmesan cheese. The amounts and cooking time are general guidelines only. Experiment with this recipe. The finished consistency should be dense and heavy.

Coat a small baking pan or dish with nonstick cooking spray. Mix 1 cup of cornmeal, one egg, 1/2 cup of milk (skim is fine), and 2 jars of meat-flavored baby food. Cook at 350 degrees for 30-40 minutes. Insert a knife into the center to check for doneness. It should come out clean. Let the brownies cool and cut into small squares. Keep refrigerated.

Many owners are surprised by their dogs' preferences in foods. For example, some dogs really enjoy fruits and vegetables. These are especially good for overweight dogs or dogs who gain weight quickly. My dogs adore seedless grapes and frozen green beans (still in their icy state). They also love apples, bananas, raisins, carrots, and peas. Be creative in trying new and different food reinforcers.

Remember to cut down slightly on the portions for your dog's regular meals when training with food. You want him to be slightly hungry so that the food reinforcers are motivating. Also, you don't want him to become overweight, which is bad for his health.

If your dog is on a special or restricted diet you can use his regular food as a reinforcer. Rather than feeding him from a bowl use his food for his daily training. All food comes directly from you during training sessions. This is also a great way to bond with your dog and form a close relationship. Having you, rather than a bowl, as a food source makes a big impression on most dogs. I always recommend that puppy owners hand-feed at least part of their dogs' meals as well.

TOYS and GAMES

In addition to using food as a primary reinforcer, toys and games are often desired by dogs. Whether toys and play are motivating or not is very individual. It takes some time getting to know a particular dog to learn what 'turns him on'.

A jackpot can be very effective in marking a 'special' training moment.

Toys

Go to any pet store or look through any pet products catalog and you will see hundreds of toys. Many pets have a wide variety of toys available, yet don't play with any of them. Others become obsessed with one particular toy above all others. Still others may play briefly with any new toy, then abandon and ignore it. When considering toys to be used as training reinforcers, it is important to keep a couple of issues in mind.

1. Some dogs have more natural 'toy drive' than others. They seem born with a desire to explore and play. Certain breeds, such as Retrievers and Border Collies, are more likely to display this tendency. These dogs are usually very interested in chasing and carrying objects

like tennis balls or fleece toys. This type of dog is easy to train using toys.

2. Familiar, readily available toys are often boring. All those toys scattered on the floor of your living room floor don't hold much interest for your dog. They are always there, just part of the background. Restricting access to certain toys makes them seem more desirable. Whenever something is scarce, it is seen as more valuable. This is true for dogs as well as for people!

Some possible training toys include:
    Tennis balls (especially those attached to ropes)...
    Fuzzy, squeaky toys (mice, hedgehogs, etc.)
    Fleece toys (chew man)...
    Kong toys...
    Braided rope toys...
    Rubber balls...

In addition to these possibilities, you might want to experiment with some more unusual toys. My Papillon loves a cat toy I bought on sale for 80 cents. It is a 2 foot flexible wand that has leather fringe on the end. You wave it around and the fringe jumps and dances. Copper loves to chase it and leap at it. It's not very sturdy and would be destroyed by larger dogs, but it's perfect for a small one.

Increasing your dog's desire for particular toys can be done by restricting access. First, choose a training toy. Then, play with it in front of your dog. You'll need to act like a fool for this. Jump around, toss the toy and catch it, and pretend you're having the best time ever.

When your dog shows some interest put the toy away. Do this 3-4 times a day, always putting the toy away without letting your dog play with it. After a couple of days you might allow your dog to sniff the toy before you put it away. Over time, your dog should become very interested in the mysterious object that you are having so much fun playing with. The only time your dog should have access to a training toy is when he is being reinforced. If you have followed this process and your dog still isn't interested in a particular toy, then it's time to try something else. Some dogs love fuzzy, furry toys while others are obsessed by chasing balls. Keep working to find something your dog really loves.

A toy reinforcer can be used in the same way that a food reinforcer is. Once the dog behaves in a desired way you can click, then allow the dog a chance to play with the toy for a very short period of time. If your dog does not want to return the toy, you will need to teach him a 'trade' cue (later in the book) and keep him on leash for more control.

SAFETY NOTE: Be particularly aware of safety issues when choosing toys for your dog. Some dogs, particularly those who are powerful chewers, can be very quick to destroy and/or consume toys. Be very careful when introducing new toys and don't allow your dog unsupervised access to them.

For example, my dogs seem to love to chew on empty plastic water bottles. I will allow them very quick access to a water bottle as a reinforcer. They can get in a few good crunches. However, I have to be sure to take it back quickly or my guys would eat pieces of it.

Games

From the moment you get your dog or puppy you should play games with him. Dogs have definite play preferences. Some adore chasing and retrieving; others love tugging. The type of play that is appropriate for each dog depends on individual temperament and personality. Vigorous physical games can be inappropriate for dogs who lack self-control or the ability to calm down quickly. If your dog gets too cranked up and can't settle down again, stick to the calmer, quieter games. Also, very rowdy games can be too much for younger puppies and adolescent dogs. They may start to nip and bite in their excitement. It's better to encourage more controlled, quieter play with these dogs.

Retrieving. Retrieving objects can be an enjoyable activity for many dogs. It is also a great way to help your dog get enough physical exercise. However, some dogs may need a bit of guidance so that the game can be fun for everyone involved. It is common for a dog to chase a thrown object, then to either lose interest when it stops moving, or to play 'keep away' with the owner. We want to encourage the dog to take the object in his mouth and to return it to you so that the game can continue.

You can start to teach the dog this concept by playing the 'two treats' game with him. You'll need some large treats that are easy to see and that roll well. Planter's cheese balls are great for this (plus, most dogs love them!) Show your dog one of the treats and throw it, encouraging him to chase it. Once he catches and eats the treat, call his name and show him the other treat, throwing it in the opposite direction. Continue throwing treats to one side, then the other, with your dog running past you in the middle. This game puts you at the center of the action. Once your dog understands and enjoys this game, you can move to the 'two toys' game. It is played in exactly the same way with two identical toys. Throw one toy and encourage your dog to chase it. When he picks it up show him the second toy and throw it in the opposite direction. Most dogs will start chasing the second toy and drop the first. Then you pick up the dropped toy and continue the game. Once your dog plays the 'two toys' game you can introduce the 'treat retrieve' and 'fetch for food' concepts. For a treat retrieve toss out a favorite treat and encourage your dog to chase and catch it. Click as he approaches and eats the treat. Then call him back to you and click and treat when he returns. Most dogs love this game because it combines both chasing and eating. For the fetch for food throw a favorite toy and, once your dog picks it up, call him to you while showing him a treat. He only gets the treat if he brings the toy back.

Tug of war. Tug of war is an appropriate game for some dogs, but not for others. If you do play tug with your dog you will need to teach him to let go of the object when you ask. You can teach an 'out' or 'release' cue by suddenly offering a really tasty smelly treat during tug play. Simply let go of the tug object and put the treat right on your dog's nose. You need to let go so that you have released pressure, then your dog can do likewise. When he lets go of the object give him the treat, pick up the object, and start playing again. The ability to have your dog let go of the object on cue puts you in charge of the game.

Find it. The 'find it' game teaches your dog how to use his amazing scenting abilities in a fun way. It's easiest to teach this game if you start with a Kong toy with some peanut butter or cheese inside. Show it to your dog, let him sniff it, then hide it as he watches (around a corner or behind a piece of furniture). Move your dog slightly away from the object, then encourage him to 'go find'. He'll probably do this very easily. Let him lick out the goodies and refill the Kong toy and start the game again. You can hide the toy in more and more difficult places as your dog gets the idea of using his nose to sniff it out.

Many dogs make up their own games to play. My business partner, Liz, has a Collie named Rhin. Rhin loves to play the 'foot' game. As you walk he will 'attack' your ankles. He's very gentle and never nips, but gives little play growls as he vigorously nudges and noses your socks. My Golden Retriever, Sully, loves to play the 'pinchy, pinchy' game. He hops up and down on his front feet (never jumps on me) as I try to pinch him (gently of course) on the shoulders and back.

LIFE REWARDS

Sometimes a reinforcer for a particular behavior is readily available in the environment. If you think about the immediate consequences of a behavior, you can often use them as reinforcers. You need to think about what your dog wants in any particular situation, then make getting that contingent on doing something that you want.

For example, when you bring out your dog's leash, he might begin leaping around in anticipation and excitement. This is a perfect training opportunity. What does your dog want? He wants you to put on the leash so he can go somewhere. You can use this to your advantage. The leash will only go on when your dog does something you want. In this case, a 'sit' would be appropriate. So you will use the reinforcement of attaching the leash when your dog sits.

Imagine the scenario: You bend over, leash in hand. Your dog leaps around wildly. Now, you should stand up straight and simply wait. Eventually, your dog will sit, possibly after trying many other things. Your job is to be patient and wait. Once your dog sits, bend over to attach the leash again. If your dog moves, stand up straight and wait. Think of it as a little dance. Your dog moves and you stop. Your dog sits still and you move. You will only attach the leash once your dog sits. After the first few sessions, your dog will get the idea. Soon, he will sit when you bring out the leash. By following this process you're using a reinforcer available in the environment.

Once your dog understands some basic obedience exercises, you can ask for those and then use life rewards as a consequence. If your dog brings you his favorite toy to throw you can ask him to 'down' first, then throw the ball for him. You've reinforced him for complying with your request. These simple little exercises can have a profound effect on your dog. He's learning that, in order to gain access to the things he wants, he needs to pay attention to you and do the things you ask.

Any activity that your dog needs or desires can serve as an effective life reward. Things as common as going outside, getting dinner, and taking a walk can be used to reinforce desirable behaviors. Your dog's 'job' is to do the simple things that you ask in order to gain access to the things he wants.

What Does YOUR Dog Want?

Before you start clicker training you should sit down and think about what your dog wants from you. There are many, many possible reinforcers out there. Your dog's desire for all these things is not equal, she will have preferences. In order to train effectively, you need to be aware of the choices your dog would make, given the opportunity.

First, make a list of 10 possible reinforcers for your dog. Be specific. Don't just say "food", name an exact type of food. Try to have no more than 5 of your 10 items be food. Also

What does YOUR
dog want?

list toys, games, and activities. Now, look closely at your list and rank order them in the way you think your dog would.

Here is my list for Copper, the Papillon:
1. Playing with his Corgi-friend Buddy.
2. Playing with the fuzzy, squeaky buzzard toy.
3. Chasing a tennis ball.
4. Peanut butter stuffed Kong.
5. String cheese.
6. Running in the big field.
7. Microwaved hot dogs.
8. Barking!
9. Getting a shoulder massage
10. Chewing on bones.

Your dog's list may look very different from this one. Try offering your dog a choice of two toys, treats, etc. and see which he chooses first. Once you have compiled your list, consider how you can use your reinforcers in a quick and efficient manner. For example, some of Copper's reinforcers can only be used at the end of a training session or in a specific place (running in the big field, chewing on a bone). However, many others can be presented and used quickly (barking, a shoulder massage, string cheese).

It is easy to become predictable and boring with your reinforcers. With my oldest dog, Katie, I got into the habit of using food almost exclusively as a reinforcer. It was simply easier (Katie would work for pocket lint!), and I wasn't thinking about the future consequences too much. Katie's motto is definitely "will work for food." While she enjoys play and toys, she is not satisfied with them as reinforcers during training because I didn't use them often enough in our early sessions.

II. Secondary Reinforcers — My Favorite Things are on the Way!

Secondary (also called conditioned) reinforcers are things that have been repeatedly paired with primary ones. Your dog learns that the secondary reinforcement signals the appearance of the primary one. As discussed earlier, dogs are capable of learning associations between stimuli by way of classical conditioning. These associations are useful because they help the dog predict events. If one event routinely follows another, the world is more understandable for the dog. And dogs, like people, feel secure when the world seems orderly and they can predict the appearance of certain events.

Cues & Signals

Cues and signals that predict events are a natural part of our environment. We have learned that a ringing phone almost always predicts that someone who wants to talk to us is calling. A knock on the door predicts that someone is waiting to be let inside. Screeching car brakes predict the possibility of danger. The sound of thunder rumbling predicts the possibility of a rainstorm.

Our dogs also learn many cues and signals in the course of day to day living. Your dog may have learned that the sound of the refrigerator door opening signals the possible availability of food. He has probably learned that the sound of jingling car keys signals the possibility of a car ride. He may have learned that the garage door opening signals the appearance of a family member. In addition to naturally-occuring relationships, we can deliberately teach our dogs specific secondary reinforcers that will predict the appearance of desirable primary ones.

Clickers

In recent years, many dog trainers have discovered the value of using a clicker as a secondary reinforcer. If the clicker is systematically presented right before a primary reinforcer, your dog will quickly learn to love hearing the clicker, as it predicts the appearance of something good. In order to teach your dog the association between the sound of the click and the primary reinforcer, you simply need to pair them together over a number of trials. This is called 'clicker conditioning' or 'charging the clicker'. You click first, then give a treat immediately after.

It doesn't take very long for most dogs to learn the 'click signals treat' connection. This connection will be learned easily and will remain strong if it is highly predictable; if the click precedes the presentation of the treat most of the time. It will deteriorate if it is not highly predictable. For example, if you click often but do not treat, the click will become much less meaningful to your dog. It would be similar to the phone ringing, but nobody being on the line most of the time. You might just start to ignore the ringing, as it is no longer very predictive.

Verbal Secondaries

Many people express the desire to use a word to mark appropriate behavior and to signal the availability of a primary reinforcer. They might state that a clicker is not always at hand or that it is awkward for them to use one. I use a verbal secondary reinforcer IN ADDITION to the clicker, NOT instead of it. The verbal can be used most successfully AFTER the initial stages of training. For the learning phase, the clicker is definitely more effective. It is clearer, and it is more precise, than a verbal secondary. However, the verbal secondary reinforcer can be used to successfully maintain the already-learned behaviors. It

can also be used in situations where the clicker is not available or appropriate.

You should take great care in choosing an appropriate verbal secondary reinforcer. You want to make sure that you use a word that is short, clear, and distinct. Also, you want it to be a word that you don't use in casual conversation or day to day interactions. I use the word "Yes!" said very distinctly and emphatically. The tone and inflection are very different from the way I would normally say the word. I've also heard people use "Great!" and "Bingo!" as secondary reinforcers. Debi Davis, a service dog trainer from Arizona, uses the word "Chip!" for one of her dogs, as it is not likely to be commonly used otherwise. The word "good" is a poor choice as it is commonly used in addressing many dogs. The verbal secondary needs to be special and unusual so it will be noticed immediately.

The verbal secondary should be as consistent in sound as possible from one time to the next. It is very hard to keep our voices the same, but the sound should vary as little as possible.

If you are training more than one dog you may want to consider whether it would be best to use the same verbal secondary for all dogs, or to use a unique word for each dog. The advantage of using the same word is that you are more likely to respond quickly and less likely to get confused and use the wrong word. Since I sometimes have trouble keeping my dogs' names straight, I use a single word. The advantage of using different words for different dogs is that your dog will not be confused about who you are reinforcing. Imagine that you have three dogs doing three different things when they hear the verbal secondary. One dog is barking at the door, one is digging in the garbage, and one is sitting looking at you adoringly. If all three hear the same verbal secondary (even though you were only addressing the one who was sitting and looking at you) they may all believe that they are being reinforced for what they are doing at that moment.

It is important to remember that the verbal secondary reinforcer is NOT praise. It is a marker for the appropriate behavior, and a signal that the primary reinforcer will now be delivered. You must not use the verbal secondary unless you offer a primary reinforcer immediately after.

• KEY CONCEPT: *The verbal secondary reinforcer is NOT praise.*

You will condition the verbal secondary in the same way that you condition the clicker. Give the verbal, then the primary. Repeat the process until your dog seems to recognize the importance of the secondary reinforcer.

III. Environmental Management — I'm in Charge Here!

We are able to train our dogs successfully because we control all the things that they would like to have. That gives us wonderful leverage when dealing with our dogs. However, many people seem to have lost the feeling of being in control. They don't understand how to structure the environment to give them the advantage in dealing with their dogs. Instead, the dog seems to be running the show, or running wild, as the individual case may be. When people call me their number one request is to help them find a way to "make the dog listen to me." Their number one problem, according to enrollment form information that clients provide, is "out of control".

Physical and Psychological Control

Let's examine some concepts of control first. There are actually two main types of control, physical and psychological. If we neglect one or the other when dealing with our dogs, we will have problems in training. Physical control involves the ability to change the dog's behavior using our own physical strength, along with the use of external devices to make that control easier. For example, to keep a dog from running into the street we would probably use a collar and a leash along with our physical ability to hold the leash without dropping it. Therefore, this control has two physical components, the collar & leash (external devices) and our own physical strength. You may have trouble keeping the dog from running into the street if either part of this physical control fails. First, your external devices could fail or could be ineffective. Second, you might not have the physical strength and motor skills necessary.

For example, imagine that Emma, an 85-year-old woman, has a young Airedale Terrier named Jake, who weighs about 65 pounds. Emma uses a quick release snap collar and a chain leash when trying to walk Jake. Being a young, strong, exuberant dog, Jake pulls when walking. The chain leash is hard for Emma to grip. Even with an appropriate leash, Emma doesn't have the strength to hold onto a bouncing, pulling Jake. The quick release collar snaps. Jake is gone. The external devices used for control failed, as did the attempt at using physical strength.

How could the outcome have been different? We cannot change Emma's physical strength. Knowing that, we have to work around it. We could provide Emma with more appropriate tools. A head halter rather than a quick release snap collar would give her much more control and be safer. (More on specific types of equipment coming up.) A leather or cotton leash would allow for a much better grip than a chain one. However, even with more appropriate control devices, there is still a major problem. Emma is relying on physical methods to control her dog, and she will never be stronger than Jake.

Training methods based mainly on attaining physical control will usually not be successful. Reliance on special equipment or physical strength is likely to fail at some point. The dog quickly learns to distinguish between those times when he must listen (the leash and collar are on and Dad is holding the leash) and those times when he is operating on his own (running loose down the street and a child is calling) and not under direct physical control.

Even with an appropriate leash, Emma doesn't have the strength to hold onto Jake.

• KEY CONCEPT: *Training methods based only on physical control will usually not be successful.*

Perhaps we could help Emma by giving her some psychological control over Jake as well. In psychological control, we work on convincing the dog that doing what we want is also in his best interest. Psychological control can seem to take longer to attain than physical control, but it is much more useful. Dogs who are only under physical control tend to revert to undesired behaviors as soon as possible. Dogs who are under psychological control exhibit more stable long-lasting behavioral change.

To gain psychological control we must train our dogs. It's that simple and that complicated.

We must train in ways that are easy and effective, and that training has to be in place in order to avoid problems like Emma's. Gaining psychological control is not a quick fix, instead it is a permanent solution for many behavior problems. Psychological control is gained over time and it takes knowledge and effort on the part of the owner.

In the short term, a collar and leash and physical strength may be necessary to keep a dog safe and close to you. However, they are simply temporary tools to be used for control until the dog has been trained. After that, the collar and leash may be necessary to comply with laws and to avoid unexpected mishaps (like that instinctive response to a squirrel running across the street), but in general they should become superfluous.

You can gain psychological control through your interactions with your dog, your training sessions, and your reinforcement history. Reinforcement history refers to the building of a mutually satisfying working relationship with your dog. It is a relationship in which he learns that working for you is the best way to get what he wants. It also refers to your dog coming to trust that you are predictable and understandable in your dealings with him. Building a reinforcement history also refers to teaching your dog that you control absolutely all the good things in the world. A dog with a strong reinforcement history is unlikely to go looking elsewhere for the things he wants. He has learned to wait for you to provide them.

You can begin to establish psychological control at any point in your dog's life. Even if you had a bad beginning, you can make changes starting right now. Your dog's behavior, and your relationship with your dog, can always be improved. A good way to begin is to establish control over your dog's environment.

Environmental Control

Environmental control (often called management by clicker trainers) bridges both the physical and psychological realms. It can involve the use of direct physical contact, but it also encompasses changes in your dog's immediate living conditions and situations, and changes in the way you relate to your dog.

So, the use of the appropriate leash and collar can be considered good management. If you have a dog who jumps on guests when they enter your home, putting on a leash before opening the door is a management technique. It won't bring about a long-lasting change in your dog's behavior, but it is effective for the short-term. Another way to manage the same problem is to crate your dog before guests enter. This changes the immediate situation for your dog and prevents the unwanted behavior. If you only have guests infrequently, or your dog weighs less than ten pounds, or your guests don't mind being jumped on, or you want to discourage people from visiting, you may only need occasional short-term management solutions. However, if you want to permanently solve the jumping problem, you will need to combine short-term management techniques with positively based training sessions.

Environmental management can involve direct control of your dog's movements. If you have a dog who chews and is destructive, you can manage the problem by preventing your dog free access to your home and possessions. Your dog can't chew on your bed pillows if he isn't allowed to roam free in the house unsupervised. You can use crating, baby gates, and closed doors to restrict his access. You can also supply appropriate chew toys and make sure your dog is getting enough physical exercise and attention (lack of these can lead to chewing problems). In a case like this, management is usually sufficient. It's impossible to teach your dog to not chew, so restricting inappropriate chewing opportunities and providing acceptable outlets for energy will decrease the probability of chewing treasured or valued objects.

Environmental management is the owner's responsibility. It places you, the owner, in a position of control. Rather than helplessly blaming your dog for acting like a normal dog (chewing, digging, barking, etc.) you start thinking about ways to manage the problem behavior by changing the situation. This is not always an easy task and may sometimes require professional advice, but it will be more successful than complaining about the dog and punishing him.

In terms of the psychological aspects of management you can think about ways to convince your dog that he needs you to obtain anything he wants. Imagine that your dog rushes through the back door, almost knocking you down in the process, whenever you let him in or out. You may decide that your dog no longer gets to go through doors unless he does so in a more controlled and careful manner. Because you have the ultimate control of the resource your dog wants (the ability to open the door for him) you can manage this situation. Begin to open the door to let your dog through, the moment he starts to rush, simply close the door and wait. When your dog settles down and is still, slowly begin to open the door again.

You will have to repeat this process for several sessions over several days. However, your dog will soon come to realize that rushing the door means he does not get to go through it. You have taken control of your dog's behavior without ever having to touch him. You've taught him that access to desired activities depends on performing specific behaviors. This is a very, very important lesson. It puts you in a position of importance for your dog. You are using psychological, rather than physical control.

Being in control of the food supply is another way to establish a psychological advantage. Whoever feeds the dog becomes a vitally important person. The food provider is to be attended to. You can use this fact to influence your dog's behavior. Don't feed your dog from a bowl. That makes the bowl, not you, important. For a few days you can carry your dog's dry food around with you in your pockets and feed him for appropriate behavior. In very short order you will have a dog who stays with you, watches you closely, and is quick to respond to your requests.

When you are dealing with canine behaviors that you would like to decrease, your first step should be to consider how you might use management to change the situation. With a little thought and creativity, you can probably design solutions to many behavior problems using physical and psychological management techniques.

KEY CONCEPTS REVISITED:

• *A reinforcer is anything that will increase the likelihood of the behavior that it follows. Primary reinforcers are often specific to a particular species, but vary between individuals. Anything that your dog wants or needs is a possible primary reinforcer.*

• *The verbal secondary reinforcer is NOT praise. A secondary reinforcer is a marker. It tells your dog that he was in the midst of a desirable behavior at the moment that he heard the mark. It is also a signal that primary reinforcement is on the way. Praise occurs after a behavior, and is meant to be pleasant in and of itself.*

• *Training methods based on physical control only will usually not be effective. It is important to establish psychological and environmental control as well. Physical control can be easily lost and then you have no back-up control. Using psychological control techniques and making environmental changes result in good overall management.*

For further reading:
How Dogs Learn *by Mary Burch, Ph.D. & John Bailey, Ph.D.*
Management Magic *by Leslie Nelson & Gail Pivar*

If you have a dog who chews and is destructive, you can manage the problem by preventing your dog free access to your home and possessions.

Chapter 4

Clicker Training Guidelines

— Getting Started —

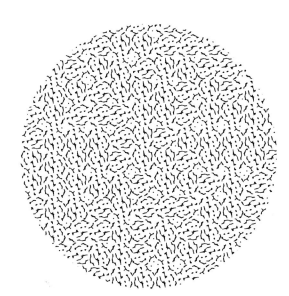

I. The Three Rules
(keeping it simple)

At first, clicker training can seem confusing and overwhelming, especially to new trainers. It involves some understanding of learning theories and principles, as well as knowledge of specific training methods and techniques. However, as with any type of learning, taking a slow, systematic step-by-step approach is best. With that in mind, start by following three simple clicker training rules.

1. Click WHILE your dog is doing something you like.
2. Always follow a click with a primary reinforcer.
3. Give the primary reinforcer as soon as possible after the click.

1. Click WHILE your dog is doing something you like. This requires three things from you as a trainer. First, you need to be prepared to capture those desirable behaviors when they occur. You should have a clicker and treats readily available, especially during the earliest stages of training. Stash clickers and treats in a number of strategic areas around the house so you can grab them quickly. You might keep them on the mantle, on a kitchen counter, on an end table in the family room, on your computer desk, etc. Keep the treats in a covered, dog-proof container! Make it a habit to carry a clicker and a few treats in your pocket. Second, you need to begin to focus on what your dog is doing right, rather than on what he is doing wrong. It is incredibly easy to ignore the good behavior and attend to the bad. This tendency needs to be reversed when clicker training. Third, you have to have good timing. Clicking too late is the biggest problem that beginning clicker trainers face. They miss their chances and end up clicking the behavior just after the one they intended. Focus on being quick to click!

2. Always follow a click with a primary reinforcer. This is a very important rule. To keep the signal the click provides clear and strong, the relationship between the two must not be broken. If the click signals the presentation of the primary reinforcer sometimes, but not others, your dog will not trust the information provided by the click. A click is a promise. Don't break that promise to your dog. If you click when you didn't intend to (and everyone does!) give the primary anyway. One mistaken click won't set back your training by much. Behaviors have to be clicked consistently in order to become habits. It's more important to keep the click as a clear signal to your dog than to make a single mistake.

3. Give the primary reinforcer as soon as possible after the click. This is very important during the initial stages of training. You don't want anything to happen between the time of the click and the presentation of the primary reinforcer. This would interfere with learning the association between the two. A good rule is that no more than 2 seconds should pass between secondary and primary reinforcers. In more advanced stages of training, once the dog clearly understands the connection between the secondary and primary reinforcers,

a bit more of a time delay can occur. For example, in early training with food treats I make sure that the treats are readily available in a pocket or container. In later stages of training I might click, then go to the other side of the room to get a treat for the dog.

By following these three rules, you can make a successful start with clicker training. Begin training one simple behavior such as looking at you (attention) or sitting. Both of these behaviors are almost always appropriate. These behaviors are also easy to observe and capture. Spend a few days just catching your dog doing one of these behaviors (no commands or cues), clicking, and treating. Notice how the behavior starts to increase. You've just started down the road to successful clicker training!

II. Making Sense to Your Dog

Try to imagine what the world must seem like from your dog's perspective. The world is populated by a large number of tall, two-legged creatures. These creatures possess some amazing abilities, such as producing food from a large white machine (refrigerator) whenever they desire. They also speak a strange language and make unusual movements and gestures with their paws (hands).

Some of these creatures are friendly and nice; while others are mean and scary. Sometimes the things you do seem to make them happy; sometimes you do things that seem to make them mad. Sometimes, they are unhappy with you or happy with you and you have no idea why. To many dogs, the world is probably a very confusing place.

Dogs are learning all the time. They try very hard to make sense of the world. Unfortunately, they are often learning things that we would rather they didn't.

An untrained dog has to work hard to figure out how to gain rewards and avoid punishments in the environment. If he isn't given any direction from the humans around him, or if that direction doesn't make sense, he's left to his own devices to figure out how to make the world work for his benefit. In cases like these, the outcomes are usually not good. In the process of learning that moving cars can hurt you, an unleashed dog may avoid tragedy for some time, but will eventually be hit and killed by a car. In trying to get attention from entering guests, an untrained dog may learn that jumping on them is the quickest way to gain that attention. Sometimes people let him jump and they play with him; sometimes people yell at him and try to shove him away. A dog trained with very strict traditional methods may learn that the best way to avoid punishments is to avoid training altogether and try to disappear when the leash and collar come out. A dog who only ever gets in the car to go to the veterinarian once a year will learn that getting in the car leads to a very bad outcome and will try to avoid that activity.

One of the most important lessons your dog can learn is that you are predictable; that you make sense. Being inconsistent in your demands and expectations is very confusing for your dog. For example, your dog cannot understand why it is OK to jump on you when you're wearing sweatpants, but not when you're wearing a suit. Or he may find it difficult to understand the difference between play wrestling with you and play wrestling with your 3-year-old nephew. Avoiding these types of inconsistencies will make it much easier for your dog to behave in the ways you desire.

When we clicker train our dogs, we are doing them a big favor because we are helping to impose some sense of order on their worlds. Clicker trained dogs learn that the world makes sense. They come to understand how to behave in ways that will bring them the reinforcers they desire. They also learn to avoid the behaviors that will lead to unpleasant consequences.

Dogs love clicker training because it gives them a way to control the environment. Your dog can make things happen by behaving in certain ways. Once your dog 'gets' the concept of clicker training, he will start acting in ways that lead to clicks and treats. This is great, because now your dog is actively seeking ways to act that are appropriate in the hopes that you will reinforce him. We tell people that at this point they have become the 'human hot dog dispenser'. Your dog has learned that he is likely to get a click and a treat for specific behaviors, and he will often try those behaviors in the hopes of being reinforced.

• KEY CONCEPT: *Clicker training gives dogs*

a way to control the environment.

People report that, once their dogs understand that they can earn reinforcement through their actions, their dogs will often try to initiate clicker training sessions. One student of mine reported that, after her first clicker training class, her dog would follow her around the house and sit in front of her, staring up at her face and wagging her tail. This is one of the great advantages of clicker training, your dog is actively engaged in the learning process and is thoroughly enjoying it.

III. Reinforce This (catching behaviors)

The first step in clicker training is to catch desirable behaviors as they occur. If you mark them with a click, then follow with a treat, those captured behaviors will be repeated.

Waiting for behaviors to occur, then marking and reinforcing them, requires patience. Many people cannot resist the desire to make something happen. They want to find some way to get the dog to behave as desired rather than to wait for the behavior to be offered. Behaviors that are freely offered are referred to as emitted behaviors by scientists. They originate from within the person or animal. Scientists use the term elicit to refer to using techniques to bring out a behavior; to make it happen. While we will use techniques to elicit behaviors during training, it is also very important to allow your dog to emit behaviors as well. If you are constantly trying to make

the dog act in specific ways, you are not giving him the opportunity to learn at his own pace and in his own way. Plus, behaviors that your dog discovers on his own tend to be stronger and longer-lasting than those you try to force on the dog.

Physically prompting and/or molding the dog into position can seem to be working at first, but it really isn't a good teaching tool. Imagine that your teacher attempted to show you how to write the alphabet by putting a hand over yours and guiding your hand to make the letters over and over. What, exactly, would you learn, and how long would it take? First, you'd learn to be very passive and allow your hand to be guided. This might take a while in the beginning, as many of us would have the tendency to stiffen, or to try to move our hands in different ways. With a little bit of time, however, you would probably learn to allow yourself to be guided. Have you learned how to write the alphabet on your own yet? No. Would you feel like you were being successful? No. If your teacher continues to guide your hand over and over you may indeed seem to be learning to write your alphabet. However, if your teacher then stops guiding you and says "write a G" you will probably be unable to do so. It would require lots and lots and lots of repetition before you might make some correct attempts at writing your alphabet on your own.

Imagine instead that your teacher sat with you and provided a pencil and paper. Whenever you attempted to write she would reinforce you. If you were motivated to work for the offered reinforcement, you would probably continue to try to write letters, working to do whatever would earn you a goodie. You would be free to write in whatever way you chose, but your teacher would only reinforce you for writing that looked like certain letters. If your teacher was able to capture you writing correctly she could shape your attempts to become letters of the alphabet (more on shaping in the next section). This would take a bit more time in the beginning, as you would have some false starts and mistakes as you learned. However, you would soon be successful. In addition to learning how to write your alphabet you would have also learned another very important lesson, that you had the ability to learn in your own way and at your own pace. You would also learn that learning is fun!

A big part of becoming a clicker trainer is being able to stand back and allow your dog to work through the learning process. Our attempts to rush in and 'help' are often counterproductive. While it might not be apparent on the outside, the dog may be starting to process information. By jumping in and offering assistance, you may actually be breaking the dog's concentration. Imagine that you are trying to concentrate on calculating your taxes and someone kept interrupting to try and hurry you along. Would that help the process? If you interrupt the learning process often enough your dog will just stop trying and wait for you to show him exactly what to do. This suppresses your dog's natural desire to learn and explore and is the very opposite of the qualities we would like

Your teacher would only reinforce you for writing certain letters...

to encourage in a clicker trained dog. In clicker training we would like our dogs to be excited and enthusiastic about learning and to be active in the process.

The best way to start practicing clicker training is to choose a behavior that your dog offers on occasion, such as lying down or sitting, and capture it with a click and treat as often as possible. Make sure it's a behavior that you want your dog to repeat. You'll see that the reinforced behavior increases dramatically over a couple of days. Does your dog perform some very cute behavior that you'd like to catch? Maybe he sits up and begs or spins in a circle when he's excited. Be aware of when the behavior usually happens (before dinner, when you're out on a walk...) and be ready to click and treat when you see it. One client of mine noticed that her dog always stretched when she let him out of his crate in the morning. She kept her clicker and treats right by the bed and was ready to catch the stretch when it happened. She was eventually able to work this into a cute "take a bow" trick.

IV. Getting Behavior (shaping, luring, targeting)

There are three main ways to get your dog to perform behaviors. They are shaping, luring, and targeting. All three are ways to build new behaviors; to get them to happen so that you can reinforce them. There are some behaviors that you'll never be able to capture naturally as they simply don't occur, or they don't occur very often. While these techniques will help us get a behavior to occur, none of them involve physically manipulating the dog.

• *KEY CONCEPT: Shaping, luring, and targeting are three ways to build new behaviors.*

Shaping

When we practice shaping we start by catching approximations of our desired behavior rather than waiting for the completed perfect behavior to occur. Shaping involves having a mental picture not only of the desired behavior, but also of the small steps leading to that behavior. Shaping requires good timing on the part of the trainer so that you can catch those early steps that will lead to your target (final, desired) behavior. Shaping also requires patience and the ability to wait for a reinforceable behavior. Many new trainers are frustrated by this, but it is absolutely essential.

You should start practicing shaping with a simple, easily observable behavior. With my Golden Retriever, Sully, I shaped him to put his head on my leg and hold it there. The first step in shaping this behavior was to click and treat whenever Sully came close to me. After all, that was really the first requirement. If he wasn't close to me, he couldn't put his head on my leg. So I would click and treat Sully for coming closer and closer to me. Once Sully seemed to understand this idea, I escalated my requirements and waited for him to move his head anywhere close to my leg before I would click and treat. At this point I wasn't expecting him to put his head on my leg, or even very close, but just that his head was in some sort of proximity to my leg. Sully tried a few other behaviors, but found with some experimentation that the only thing getting reinforced was moving his head towards my leg. Once he discovered this he focused on different head movements, again testing to see what would earn a click and a treat. I was only reinforcing movements that brought Sully's head closer and closer to my leg and ignoring everything else. Sully was free to try anything he wanted, and he did, but when something didn't pay off, he'd move back to those behaviors that did earn reinforcement.

I worked on shaping this behavior over a number of short sessions. You shouldn't expect your dog to 'get it' right away. With each new session I'd go back and reinforce an easier version of the behavior a few times to help him get started. For example, if we ended a session with Sully putting his head one inch away from my leg I'd start the next session by clicking and treating any head movement within six inches of my leg a few times, then raise the requirements slowly.

There is no way to write out a step-by-step cookbook approach to shaping any particular behavior. This is because shaping proceeds differently for every dog and for every behavior being trained. Shaping is an interactive process between the trainer and the dog. You have to be very observant in order to catch approximations of the target behavior. You also have to have good timing so that you are actually clicking the intended behaviors. Finally, you have to be very good at 'reading' your dog — knowing when to hold off and wait for your dog to offer more and knowing when to accept the offered behaviors. Shaping is a skill that requires practice for both the subject and the trainer.

In Karen Pryor's clicker training classic 'Don't Shoot the Dog' she describes shaping in an exercise that she calls the training game. The training game is a fun and easy way to practice shaping. You can start by shaping human subjects, then moving on to animal ones. In my psychology classes we do training game demonstrations as part of the material on Learning Theories. We start with two volunteers, one the trainer and the other the subject. The subject leaves the room while the class decides on a behavior for the trainer to shape. It's best to start with simple, easy to observe behaviors like turning in a circle,

lifting your arms over your head, turning the lights on and off, or sitting in a specific chair. When the subject returns to the room he or she is told to listen for the clicks (which mean 'you're right'). It is the trainer's job to mark behaviors that will lead the subject to perform the target behavior. If the target behavior was turning off the lights the trainer would click whenever the subject moved towards the area of the light switch. Then she would click for being close to the light switch. Then she would click for moving a hand; then for moving a hand towards the light switch. At this point most subjects do the next natural thing, switch the light switch off. At each step in the shaping process, the trainer might reinforce at that level anywhere from one to ten times before requiring more.

When working with human subjects we click, but don't give the treat right away. This is something I would never, ever, do with an animal subject. Animals must receive their primary reinforcers right away. However, we tell the human subject that his or her goodies (usually small candies) will be stockpiled for the end of the game. This helps the game to move along faster as the subject isn't moving back to the trainer after each click for a treat.

When playing the training game with humans I have seen cases where the subject seems to get stuck. Instead of trying different behaviors, the person starts trying to figure out what to do next. This is when I tell people "don't think, just act". Human beings tend to get caught up in the cognitive process of solving the shaping puzzle. Often they get stuck when they start thinking "now what is it my trainer actually wants me to do?" I tell subjects to go back to the last behavior that earned a click and continue from there. Animals actually find shaping much easier as they are more likely to try lots of different actions and not get caught up in the thought process.

Something interesting that I have noticed in working with humans playing the training game is that, when given a choice, people almost always want to be the trainer rather than the subject. In considering this phenomenon it seems to me that, in general, people like to be in control of situations. Being the trainer seems like a position of control. Being the subject means that you have to give up any sense of control. It takes a measure of trust in order to give that control to someone else. You need to believe that your trainer will be fair and will not hurt you. Every trainer should have the experience of being the subject in the training game. It is an important lesson in understanding how your dog feels during training. If a session has been difficult for the subject, he or she can identify with the dog's feelings of frustration and uncertainty. Completely relying on someone else for information on behaviors that will lead to reinforcement can be a true learning experience that will make you a better trainer.

The term click-wise dogs refers to dogs who have had experience with and understand clicker training. The click-wise dog has learned the meaning of the sound of the click (that's right! & a goodie is coming now). He also understands how to play the training game. He has learned that trying new behaviors during shaping can lead to reinforcement. He is comfortable trying out new things until he hits on the right one. A click-wise dog has learned how to learn. This is a very important foundation step that needs to be considered. A dog who is naive (new to clicker training) may be slow to try new behaviors. During shaping, he may sit and stare at you for long periods of time, or he may wander away if nothing happens (no clicks & treats) for a while. It will take your dog some time to learn the rules of this new kind of training, so be patient. Make success very easy for your dog to achieve. Your shaping should proceed in tiny steps with lots of reinforcement along the way.

Often, dogs develop behaviors known as default behaviors. A default behavior is the one the dog reverts to whenever he is unsure of what is expected. Usually, a default behavior is the first behavior that you taught using the clicker. Often, this is a sit. The dog seems to fixate on that behavior. It made a huge impression as it was his first experience with clicker training. It was the first action that clearly earned him reinforcement. You'll find that when you get out the clicker and treats your dog will start to offer his default behavior. If you don't want the default behavior, you will need to wait until your dog does something else, then reinforce that. As long as the new behavior isn't anything you really don't want your dog to do, like barking, reinforce anything other than the default behavior. This will help your dog to understand that other things will also earn reinforcement.

You might work on a creativity session or two to help your dog understand that there are lots of possible behaviors that will be reinforced if they are offered. During a creativity session you will click and treat any behavior that is different from the last one. Rather than getting your dog to fixate on a particular action, you are encouraging him to try a number of things. This is part of your dog's learning how to learn process. If your dog shuts down and doesn't offer much in the way of different behaviors this is an excellent exercise. For example, if your dog simply sits and stares at you, smile pleasantly and watch closely for ANY behavior that you can reinforce. Your dog might shift his eyes to one side — click and treat that. He might lick his lips — click and treat that. He might shift his weight from one hip to the other — click and treat that. He might twitch his ears — click and treat that. You get the idea.

In shaping sessions we want the dog to offer lots of different behaviors so that we have a variety to choose from. Some dogs have absolutely no problem with this; they are always trying new things. In traditional forms of training these are the dogs who are hard to control, and often the most exasperating. In clicker training, these dogs are the easiest to work with as they give us a great variety of behaviors to choose from. So take heart, all of you with overactive Jack Russell Terriers and Labrador Retrievers! That constant activity level actually means that you have a

Every trainer should have the experience of being the subject in the training game.

dog who will be easier to clicker train than a quieter, more sedate animal.

A fun and interesting shaping exercise called 101 Things to Do with a Box is a great way to start clicker training. You start with a sturdy cardboard box of any size. However, make sure the size is appropriate to the size of your dog (small box for toy dogs, medium box for average size dogs, etc.) Be ready with your clicker and treats when you place the box on the floor. Click and treat your dog for ANY interaction he has with the box. Click and treat for looking at the box, for sniffing the box, for bumping it with his nose, etc. Your target behavior is 'interaction with the box in any way'.

TO PLAY 101 THINGS TO DO WITH A BOX YOU WILL NEED:

1. A sturdy cardboard box.
2. A clicker.
3. A quantity of desirable treats.
4. Your dog.
5. An open and relaxed attitude.
6. A calm non-distracting environment.

Some trainers find it difficult to engage in a training exercise that doesn't seem to have any clear-cut obvious outcome or goal. Creativity sessions and 101 things to do with a box are important for the process of actually performing them, not for the finished product. The process teaches the dog and the trainer how clicker training works. The dog learns that trying new things leads to clicks and treats. He learns to loosen up and experiment. He learns that training is fun. The trainer learns to be very observant and to catch offered behaviors. She also gets a chance to practice her timing in an exercise where the outcome isn't crucial to the dog's later behavior. If you approach these sessions with an open and enthusiastic attitude, both you and your dog will learn quite a bit from them.

If you feel ready for a more focused shaping exercise start with a very simple behavior such as your dog turning his head to look in one direction or the other. When you begin your shaping session your dog will probably start out by looking at you. You will be watching for any shift in your dog's eyes to one side or the other. Don't expect a head turn yet, just a small shift in eye focus. This is the first

behavior to click and treat. Continue to click and treat whenever your dog shifts his gaze. Soon, you should notice that he starts to move his head in the desired direction. Click and treat for this behavior. Also, click and treat if he holds his gaze in the desired direction for more than a second or two. Do NOT try to entice your dog to look in the desired direction. Your job is to wait for the behavior, then to reinforce it. It is very difficult to simply wait, but it is very important to do so. Give your dog the opportunity to learn on his own, don't try to 'help' him. Be quiet and don't move around. Just click whenever he performs a behavior that will lead to him turning his head to the side.

In your shaping sessions you will probably start to realize that your timing is a little slow. Sometimes you might be aware that you have completely missed a perfect opportunity to reinforce. If you notice this, it is good because it means you are becoming aware of 'clickable' behaviors. Don't worry unduly about these missed opportunities. Another chance to click will occur. Be pleased that you are able to 'see' those desirable behaviors, even if you are a bit late. Most of us have less than perfect timing, and we all miss behaviors we should have clicked from time to time. With practice, you will get better. Being aware that you missed a good chance to click is the first step in recognizing your dog performing in desirable ways. Be pleased that you are aware of this and continue practicing your shaping skills.

With some practice you can significantly improve your timing. Denise Nord, a clicker trainer and clicker class instructor from Minnesota, shared a class demonstration idea with me, and it is a great way to improve timing. This is usually performed in a class setting, but could be practiced with an informal group of owners/trainers. Trainers are provided with clickers. The instructor tosses a stuffed toy (we use a dolphin called 'Flipper') into the air. Trainers are instructed to click when the toy is at the highest point of his 'jump'. Within a few trials, most trainers are able to click at the appropriate time. You can add a number of variations to this including having trainers click when the toy hits the ground and clicking when it is even with a certain level (such as a counter or tabletop) on its way down. You can even add a double-spin to the rotation and have trainers catch the second spin. It helps to have an experienced clicker trainer act as an observer to give feedback on how accurate the trainers are in their timing.

While shaping is a fun and effective way to build behaviors, there are several other important techniques that are useful as well. Both luring and targeting are more directive by showing the dog the behavior you want. Interestingly, while both techniques can seem to lead to quick progress, true understanding actually occurs more slowly. These are more passive learning methods for the dog. The dog is being shown or led rather than having a chance to discover the correct behavior on his own.

• KEY CONCEPT: *Shaping allows the dog to be an active participant in the learning process.*

Luring

Usually, luring is accomplished using a small tidbit of food. For some dogs, a favorite toy can work as a lure as well. The easiest way to describe luring is to think of the lure as a nose magnet. The dog will naturally follow the magnet with his nose. This makes it relatively easy for the trainer to move the dog into desired positions.

Luring is most often used to help the dog make position changes with his body. In our Beginner Obedience classes, we use food lures to move the dogs into either a sit, stand, or down. We also use luring to get the dog to walk nicely next to the owner. These exercises will be described more specifically in Chapter 6 "A Basic Training Plan". In addition, luring can be useful in teaching tricks such as sit up, spin, and roll over.

The effectiveness of luring depends primarily on the owner's hand position. Since the dog's nose tends to follow the lure, in order to be successful the owner must hold the lure in the proper position. The lure needs to be exactly where you want your dog's nose to be. If it's too high, too low, or too far away, your dog will not be able to be correct.

Success in luring also depends on the treat or toy used. It must be highly desirable; something your dog is definitely willing to work for. The food should be something with a strong aroma. A couple of possibilities are freeze-dried liver (sold in most pet supply stores), bits of cooked chicken coated with garlic powder, or small pieces of strong-smelling cheese. If you use a toy as a lure, it should be small enough to fit into your hand or pocket when not in use, and easy to hold. You might try a tennis ball, braided rope tug toy, or a squeaky fuzzy stuffed animal.

Some dogs, especially those who are very food motivated, get grabby and nippy when you have a food lure in your hand. If your dog does this you can try a couple of techniques. First, keep the food in your closed fist rather than in your fingers. Your dog will still be able to smell and follow the food. Then, when you give your dog the treat open your palm up completely so your dog takes the food from your flat hand. Or, you could try putting some peanut butter on a spoon and using that as your lure, allowing your dog to lick the peanut butter as the treat.

You can work on teaching your dog to take treats gently by teaching him that grabbing makes the treat go away. Hold the treat in your hand and let your dog sniff at it. If he tries to bite at your hand move it behind your back for a moment. Don't wave your hand around, move it slowly, but deliberately. If your dog moves away from your hand then you should click and open up your hand to let him have the treat. The target behavior that you are reinforcing is moving away from the hand holding the treat, even if only slightly. Very quickly, most dogs learn a bit of self-control. They learn that, in order to get the treat, they have to back away a bit.

If you are still having nipping problems when you use food treats you might try shaping and targeting (described in the next section) rather than luring.

With luring you will use the food or toy to entice your dog to move into the desired position. Once this happens you will click and then give the treat or let the dog play with the toy for a short time. Luring relies on repetition to teach the dog to move in specific ways. Your dog learns to follow the motion of your hand as it moves. Once your dog has reliably learned to follow the lure, you can begin to 'fade' it. Fading the lure refers to the process of slowly and systematically removing the food, while continuing to use your hand motion as a signal to your dog to perform the behavior.

Fading is accomplished by mixing 'empty hand trials' with food lures. In an empty hand trial you make the same exact hand motion as you did when you had the food lure, but your hand is empty. When your dog follows the hand motion you click, then take the treat out of your pocket to give him. By randomly mixing food and non-food trials, your dog learns to follow the hand motion, not just the food. This technique makes the hand motion the signal to perform the behavior and the food follows as the primary reinforcer.

Targeting

In targeting, you will teach your dog to move towards and touch an object. You can use a number of different objects as targets. A few of the objects we use include an open hand, target sticks, plastic margarine lids and paper plates. Your hand and the sticks can be moved to different positions for your dog to follow. The lids and plates can be placed in locations that you would like your dog to move towards. It is easiest to start teaching your dog the concept of targeting by using the palm of your hand as a target. To begin, hold out your open palm with a piece of food in it. When your dog approaches your hand to take the treat, click as he eats the goodie. Move your hand slightly up, down, or to the side and repeat. After about 5 trials with food in your hand simply hold out your hand. Most likely, your dog will approach it and sniff. When he does, click and give him a treat from your other hand or pocket. Move your hand to slightly different positions, clicking and treating whenever your dog approaches. Hold your hand sideways and upside down, clicking and treating whenever he moves toward and touches your palm. Move your hand slightly over your dog's head on one trial, then lower it towards the floor on another.

Once your dog gets the idea that touching your palm will be reinforced, you can raise your requirements slightly by moving your hand a few inches as he approaches. Your dog must now follow your hand in order to touch it. This exercise can be useful for teaching your dog to walk next to you by following your hand. You can also teach simple tricks like having your dog jump up to touch the palm of your hand.

Target sticks are very popular and useful tools. The target stick can be made of wood, plastic,

Creativity sessions and 101 Things to Do with a Box are important for the process of actually performing them… not for the finished product.

or aluminum. Its length can vary, depending on your dog's size (longer for small dogs, shorter for bigger dogs). I use a 4 foot stick for my 8 pound Papillon and a 2-3 foot stick for my 65 pound Retrievers. The stick should have one end in a contrasting color. You can use non-toxic paint or a marker, or add a soft rubber tip (this is safest as it guards against possible injuries). You might put some electrical tape on the tip as well.

To begin using the target stick you will need to practice without your dog. You will need to become adept at holding and moving the stick while you also click and deliver treats. While this might seem tricky at first, it will become easier very quickly. People have many different techniques for using the target stick, but the one that follows seems to work well for most. First, grasp and hold the target stick so that you can quickly and smoothly move it to different positions around you. You will probably find a point at which the stick balances well in your hand somewhere in the upper 1/3 of the stick. Next, add the clicker to the same hand that holds the stick. You'll be holding the stick across your palm and holding the clicker between your thumb and index finger. Practice clicking the clicker while holding the stick relatively still. Once you have mastered this motor skill, you can then practice giving a treat with your free hand after you click. While this may sound complicated, it usually only takes a few minutes of practice to master. Remember to practice without your dog present until you are comfortable with the technique.

Next you will teach your dog to approach the target stick. You can accomplish this by shaping. Be ready as soon as you begin because many dogs will immediately glance at this new object in your hand. When this happens, click and treat. Try not to miss this first opportunity. Any interest in the stick, at all, should be reinforced. Don't wait for the final target behavior (approaching and touching the stick). This is asking too much for most dogs. Instead, progress in tiny little baby steps towards your goal. At first, reinforce your dog for glancing at the stick, then for any slight move in the general direction of the stick, then for a more deliberate approach, etc. Your target behavior is for your dog to approach and touch the end of the stick with his nose.

If your dog acts as if the stick is invisible you may need to give him some help getting started. You can move the stick slightly to attract his attention, but don't wave it around wildly! You are going to want your dog to learn to approach the stick when it is held still, so keep movement minimal at first. If your dog still doesn't show any interest in the stick you can 'bait' it on the end with a dab of peanut butter or a bit of cheese. When your dog approaches the stick you can click and let him have the goodie on the end. Only 'bait' the stick a few times. After that, wait and give your dog a chance to investigate the stick on his own, being ready to reinforce for any interest.

Work on teaching your dog to approach the target stick in very short sessions. It's much better to do 5 quick 2-minute sessions than to do one 10-minute session. Dogs seem to learn best with more frequent, shorter training trials. Take breaks between each session and you will get the best results. When you go back for each new session temporarily lower your standards for reinforcement. For example, if you ended your last session with your dog approaching and touching the stick, start your next session by reinforcing you dog for simply approaching the stick. After reinforcing several times for easier versions of the behavior you can then increase your requirements and continue your progress.

An example of your shaping plan for teaching your dog to touch the end of the target stick might look like this:

1. Dog glances at stick, CT (click & treat).
2. Dog moves slightly towards stick, CT.
3. Dog makes more movement towards stick, CT.
4. Dog deliberately approaches stick, CT.
5. Dog moves nose close to stick, CT.
6. Dog sniffs stick, CT.
7. Dog touches stick (anywhere) with nose, CT.
8. Dog touches lower half of stick with nose, CT.
9. Dog touches lower third of stick with nose, CT.
10. Dog touches end of stick with nose, CT.

You would reinforce at any specific level anywhere from 2-10 times before moving on. If your dog seems to get stuck at a level you should move backwards and make it easier for him to earn reinforcement, then try moving ahead again.

In working with the target stick it is also important to hold the stick in different positions around you and your dog. You should move it to slightly different places (in front of you, to one side or the other, slightly raised, slightly lowered, etc.) between trials. You want your dog to approach and touch the stick regardless of its position.

When using other types of targets you will follow the same training pattern. Once your dog has learned to approach and touch one object, he will usually learn the others very quickly. For moveable targets like margarine

lids and plates you can teach your dog to touch them up close, then slowly move them further and further away from you and your dog. Your dog will have to move away from you to touch the target. Targets can be placed on the floor, on a chair, or even taped to a wall.

Target training is a very valuable foundation tool for more advanced training. It can be used to train tricks, advanced obedience exercises, and agility (more on these in upcoming chapters). It is a good idea to introduce the concept of targeting early in your training.

KEY CONCEPTS REVISITED:

• *Clicker training gives dogs a way to control the environment. Dogs learn, through consistent clicker training, that the world is an orderly and predictable place. They learn that behaving in desirable ways leads to good consequences. By teaching your dog this basic concept, you are giving him a way to control his world. He can 'make' you click and treat, by doing things that you want. You now have a dog who will spend his time trying to figure out how to get reinforced, rather than spending his time looking for trouble.*

• *Shaping, luring, and targeting are three ways to build new behaviors. In the past, animals trainers have used a number of methods to compel their subjects to behave in certain ways. Clicker trainers want to get behaviors while avoiding the use of physical force and coercion. The techniques of shaping, luring, and targeting provide gentler methods for training new behaviors.*

• *Shaping allows the dog to be an active participant in the learning process. Of all the possible methods for getting a dog to perform new behaviors, shaping allows the dog the most freedom and control. In shaping, the trainer allows the dog to behave in any way he wishes, and marks those behaviors he or she finds appropriate with a click and a treat. The dog discovers what will be rewarded by trying out a number of different behaviors.*

For further reading/viewing:
Clicker Training for Dogs *by Karen Pryor*
Clicker Magic (video) *by Karen Pryor*
Clicker Fun: Click & Go (video) *by Deborah Jones, Ph.D.*

Target training is a very valuable tool for more advanced training.

Chapter 5

Puppy Stuff

— Getting a Good Start —

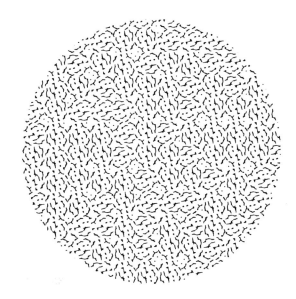

A good beginning can make all the difference between having a wonderful lifelong companion and having constant frustrations and upsets, which often leads to the dog leaving the home. My main goal as an obedience class instructor, particularly in puppy class, is to keep dogs in their homes. Once they leave their first homes, many dogs eventually end up in shelters and may even be euthanized. Even nice, adoptable dogs can be euthanized simply due to lack of space and funds. This is not to say that there are no circumstances under which an owner should find a new home for a puppy or dog, just that the original home is often the best. Usually, the current owners already have an emotional attachment to the puppy or dog, and are willing to put forth some effort in order to make the relationship work. Subsequent owners may not feel this attachment and may not be motivated to put in as much effort.

Puppy classes are becoming increasingly popular among both obedience trainers and pet owners. Happily, many people are beginning to understand the importance of getting off to a good start. Puppies are like human infants in many ways. They have special needs and require an enormous amount of energy and patience. Left to their own devices, they will find trouble. They need constant supervision. In addition, early experiences can have a lifelong effect on their behavior. Smart owners realize, early on, that they need professional and knowledgeable advice on how to best deal with their puppies. Puppies have some predictable problems at different stages in their development. By starting early, owners can learn how to deal with these issues in gentle, positive and effective ways.

I. Clicker Training for Puppies

Clicker training for puppies should be introduced as soon as possible. Any puppy old enough to go to a new home (at least 7 weeks of age) is old enough to learn the click/treat connection. There's a common myth that dog training should not start until the puppy is at least 6 months old. That myth comes from the days when training techniques were very harsh. Young puppies couldn't stand the pressure and physical compulsion involved. With kinder, gentler methods, we can begin training the moment we meet our puppies. Since our puppies are always learning, we need to teach them the things we want them to know (sit, come when called, walk nicely on a leash), rather than letting them learn the wrong things (jump, nip, destroy).

KEY CONCEPT: *Puppies are always learning. It's up to us to teach them the things we want them to know.*

When first teaching young puppies about clicker training, you can click then give them a lick of canned dog food or meat-flavored baby food from your finger.

II. Puppy Problems

Some common issues and challenges that puppy owners face include: housetraining, nipping, jumping, chewing and high activity levels. These issues can be present in older dogs as well, and the same advice as given below would apply. However, puppy owners are almost guaranteed to have to deal with these problems. In dealing with puppy owners these are the issues that surface over and over again.

1. Housetraining. When a puppy has to go, He's gotta go NOW! Puppies have little to no control over their bladder and bowels. This ability comes with age and physical development. Understanding where it is appropriate to go is another matter. For the puppy, anywhere is fine. Most tend to avoid going in the places where they eat and sleep, but anywhere else is fair game.

For most of us with new puppies, housetraining is our first training challenge. We know where we want our puppies to go potty, the challenge is in helping the puppy to understand what we want. Luckily, dogs are creatures of habit. Once they have gone in the same place a few times, they tend to return there. Puppies can learn the appropriate 'potty place' through consistent repetition.

By following a few key ideas, you can accomplish housetraining with a minimum number of accidents.

First, keep your puppy under your direct supervision at all times. This is vital to avoiding accidents. If your puppy wanders out of your sight, it is very likely that he will find a quiet spot to do his business. Don't let this happen or he will get in the habit of finding unoccupied corners of the house to use. Instead, always keep the puppy close to you. He should be in the same room you are at all times. Use baby gates to close off doorways. If necessary, use an umbilical cord (a leash or length of rope that you loop around your waist and attach to your dog's collar) to keep him close by. When you cannot supervise your puppy put him in his crate (more on the specifics of crate training follows). Don't expect your roommate, children or significant other to supervise your puppy. Other people tend to 'forget' this responsibility.

Second, choose a potty place. You need to decide where you want your puppy to go and take him to that place whenever you think he needs to go potty. If your puppy will be using a fenced back yard it is important that you take him to his potty area on his leash for the first few weeks. Allow him to sniff around a limited area, but don't let him get too distracted. By having him on a leash you are keeping him from running around and playing when he should be concentrating on potty business. You MUST go out with your puppy in order to be sure that he has actually gone — yes, even in the rain or snow. Many puppies get distracted outside, come back inside, and then remember what they need to do.

If you will be walking your dog on leash while he does his business you should make 'pit stops' at the same locations on each outing and give him the opportunity to go there.

If you are eventually going to have your puppy go potty outside, then paper training is an unnecessary extra step and could be very confusing for your dog. However, if you have a dog who will be using papers indoors (usually a small dog who lives in an apartment) then you can start with papers. There is even a new 'dog litter' product on the market that is used just like cat litter. You can follow exactly the same methods for paper training or litter training as for training a dog to go outside.

Third, stick to a very strict schedule during your puppy's early weeks in your home. Eating, sleeping, exercising, play and potty times should all be frequent and predictable for the young puppy. As I stated earlier, dogs are creatures of habit. Building good habits in the beginning will pay off later. For a young puppy set up a schedule that includes 3-4 meals, play sessions, training sessions, naps and frequent potty times. Most puppies learn to adjust to their schedules very quickly.

An example of a typical schedule for a 10-week old puppy might be as follows:

7:00 a.m.	Potty time
7:15 a.m.	Breakfast
7:30 a.m.	Walk/potty time
7:45 a.m.	Training
8:00 a.m.	Play time
8:30 a.m.	Morning nap
9:30 a.m.	Potty time
9:45 a.m.	Walk

10:15 a.m.	Play time
11:15 a.m.	Potty time
11:30 a.m.	Lunch
11:45 a.m.	Potty time
12:00 p.m.	Afternoon nap #1
2:00 p.m.	Potty time
2:15 p.m.	Training
2:30 p.m.	Play time
3:30 p.m.	Walk/Potty time
4:00 p.m.	Afternoon nap #2
5:30 p.m.	Potty time
5:45 p.m.	Dinner
6:00 p.m.	Potty time
6:15 p.m.	Play time
7:00 p.m.	Walk/Potty time
7:30 p.m.	Evening nap
8:00 p.m.	Potty time
8:15 p.m.	Training
8:30 p.m.	Play time
9:00 p.m.	Potty time
9:15 p.m.	Bedtime
11:00 p.m.	Potty time
3:00 a.m.	Potty time

*Other overnight potty outings may be necessary!

Makes you tired just thinking about it, doesn't it?! But puppies do require this much time and attention. It's important to be aware of the enormous time and energy commitment a young puppy needs.

The above schedule includes 3 meals, 4 naps, 3 training sessions, 4 walks, 5 play sessions, and 14 opportunities for the puppy to go potty in an appropriate place. Some puppies may need more frequent potty breaks, more naps, more exercise, etc. You can adjust as necessary to suit the individual. As the puppy matures you can change the schedule as needed.

Fourth, choose and use a 'potty' word or phrase. Keep in mind that this is something you will have to say in public, so choose carefully. It's also important that everyone in the household use the same word or phrase. Some commonly used words and phrases are "go potty", "hurry up', "do your business", and "let's go". At first, you will use your word or phrase as your puppy is actually going. Say it very quietly, but in an encouraging voice. As soon as your pup finishes, use a verbal marker such as "Yes!" or "Great!" and give him a treat and some praise. It's important that you have treats ready in your pocket and you give one right after he has finished going. You want your puppy to make the connection between his action and the reinforcement. If you wait until you go back inside to give the treat it will be too late. At that point your puppy is being reinforced for going back into the house, not for going potty in the appropriate place.

Continue using your chosen potty word or phrase whenever your puppy is actually going potty. This connects the verbal cue to the behavior. At times in which you know your puppy is about to go potty, such as first thing in the morning, use your potty cue as your puppy is sniffing around. Remember to use a verbal marker and a treat to reinforce.

Fifth, do NOT scold or punish your puppy for having an accident. Any type of punishment will be counterproductive to your housetraining. Imagine the following scenario: You are sitting in your living room watching

TV while your puppy is happily playing with his toys. You notice that he walks over to the corner, squats, and begins to urinate. You jump up yelling "No! Bad dog! Bad, bad dog!", scoop him up and rush him outside.

A few weeks of vigilance in the beginning will yield long lasting results…

From your perspective you just punished your dog for going potty in the house. However, think about it from your puppy's perspective. Just as he's relieving himself you swoop down on him, scaring him to death. Instead of making the connection between the scolding and going in the house, he may make a connection between your presence and going potty. He may think that going potty in your presence was the mistake. Now, when you take him to the appropriate potty place he may not go for fear of getting in trouble again. This means he'll hold it until he gets back in the house and can sneak out of your sight for a second. You've created a major problem where only a small one existed before.

So what should you do instead? Certainly, if you actually catch your dog in the act of urinating in an inappropriate place you should interrupt the behavior ("oh no! not here") and take him to the appropriate place immediately. However, you don't want to be too frightening. After all, your puppy is only doing what comes naturally. In addition, you should consider any accidents your fault for not keeping a closer eye on your puppy. And it's not fair to punish your puppy for your mistakes.

If you approach housetraining in a calm and consistent manner, you will see positive results very quickly. A few weeks or months of vigilance in the beginning will yield long lasting results. Once trained, most dogs have few to no accidents throughout their lives. In an already trained adult dog one of the first signs of a possible health problem is having housetraining accidents. If this occurs, visit your veterinarian for a check-up. If you have followed all of the above suggestions and your puppy is still having accidents, or if your puppy is having accidents in his crate/bed, have your veterinarian check for a possible bladder infection. Most bladder infections are relatively mild and easily treated.

2. Nipping. Almost all puppies nip. They nip in play and in excitement. They don't distinguish between toys, other animals, and humans, they nip everyone and everything. They have razor sharp baby teeth that really

hurt! Our second big training challenge is to teach the puppy that human skin is off-limits for nipping. We are teaching them what is called 'bite inhibition' — the understanding that they must control their jaws.

The gentlest and most effective way to deal with nipping problems is with a time-out. Set up your puppy's crate so that you will have easy and quick access when needed. Whenever your puppy's teeth come into contact with your skin or clothing, he should get a 2 minute time-out. Calmly escort him to his crate, put him inside, and completely ignore him for 2 minutes, then calmly release him. The time-out will have to be consistently repeated until your puppy makes the connection that putting teeth on people always leads to this consequence. The time-out is a mildly unpleasant event for most puppies because they temporarily lose their freedom and your company.

It is very important that the time-out is conducted in a very calm and objective manner. You should not scold or correct your dog in any way other than by temporarily restricting him to his crate. This procedure works well when it is response contingent. This means that every time the behavior occurs, the response follows. It can be difficult at first to keep repeating the time-out process, but after a couple of days most puppies have decreased their nipping dramatically.

If your puppy resists going to his crate you need to be gently persistent. Don't drag your puppy, but lead him by the collar (or a short bit of rope attached to his collar for this purpose) or pick him up if necessary. He simply does not have a choice in this process. Most puppies give up resisting after the first few time-outs.

Many owners are concerned that the time-out procedure will make the puppy dislike his crate. This has not been a problem with the hundreds of puppies we've used the procedure on. If you follow the crate training guidelines for making it a comfortable and pleasant experience in general, the puppies don't dislike or avoid the crate at other times. It's the same as sending a child to his room for misbehavior. He will dislike the temporary loss of freedom, not the room itself.

Another method to use when you don't have a crate or time-out place available is to temporarily remove yourself and your attention from your dog. If you are playing with your puppy and he starts to nip you can say "Ouch!" and immediately move away and ignore your puppy for a minute or so. Then return and begin playing again, repeating the removal of yourself and your attention if his teeth touch you.

It is very important that you do not physically punish your puppy for nipping. In many cases, owners will swat at the puppy or hit him on the muzzle. This often leads to an increasingly aggressive response which can escalate into a growl, snarl, harder nip or even a full bite. High energy, excitable puppies may take your physical response as an invitation for even rougher play. Remember, you want to decrease the behavior, not increase it.

Also, it is not appropriate to play with your puppy in such a way that he becomes overly excited and agitated. Vigorous physical play such as wrestling and chasing games may be too arousing for your puppy and can lead to nipping and biting responses. Keep play at a calmer, more relaxed level.

Nipping may also be a sign that your dog needs something appropriate to chew on. See the discussion of chewing that follows for more advice.

3. Jumping. Another nearly-universal problem that puppy owners report is jumping. Usually, puppies jump on humans in the excitement of greeting after a period of separation. Because our faces are so far away from theirs they jump up to try to get closer to us. Many puppy owners create their own jumping problems because they tolerated or even encouraged jumping when the puppy was fuzzy, small and cute. Many people enjoy the excitement their puppy expresses when they return, it makes them feel good to know they've been missed. However, when the puppy becomes larger, stronger, and more persistent, they want to stop the jumping. An educated and knowledgeable puppy owner can often avoid the jumping problem by never allowing it to develop. However, once the problem occurs there are positively-based solutions.

First, keep greetings calm and relaxed. Don't work your puppy up into a frenzy when you return after an absence. Ignoring your dog for a few minutes on your return will give him a chance to adjust to your presence. Simply avoid making eye contact with your dog or bending over him for a short time upon your return. When you do greet your dog make it a quiet interaction. Keep your voice low and calm. Give your dog a few pats or a scratch behind the ear. Ask him to sit before you interact with him. You might even sit on the floor with him so he has no need to jump up to reach you. All of these small changes will serve to make the greeting less energetic and exciting, which will decrease your dog's jumping behavior.

If your dog is a confirmed jumping champion, you will need to work harder to change the behavior. First, determine the situations in which you can predict that your dog will jump. The most common ones are: 1) greeting you when you come home, 2) greeting visitors to your home, 3) greeting people outside of your home, 4) a response to exciting situations. If you can predict when jumping will occur then you can take steps to prevent it and, more importantly, to teach your dog what to do instead. You can't simply eliminate jumping, you must give your dog a more appropriate behavior to perform in its place. Most people choose sitting as an appropriate replacement for jumping. An important point to keep in mind as well is that your dog will continue a behavior as long as it is rewarded. You need to think about what it is that is leading your dog to continue jumping. What is your dog gaining from the behavior? You have to find a way to eliminate the reward.

One method for decreasing jumping behavior is to play 'invisible dog'. Simply pretend that your puppy does not exist when he is jumping. Do not look at him, talk to him, or acknowledge him in any way. This is relatively easy with a small puppy, much harder with a grown dog, especially a large one. Your puppy is invisible unless he has all four feet on the floor. Then he becomes visible and you give him praise and attention. If he starts to jump again, he becomes invisible once more. This is a simple method to understand and use, especially for children.

If your puppy jumps on people who approach him you can enlist some friends and relatives to help you practice 'walk-aways'. To begin, have your puppy on leash and have a person approach. Your job is to simply stand still and hold the leash. Do not talk to the puppy or pull on the leash. As the person approaches and the puppy starts to jump instruct the person to turn and walk away. The person should walk away a few steps, then turn and approach again if the dog keeps his feet on the floor. Repeat this technique as often as necessary. Over a few trials you should see the person being able to get closer and closer before the puppy starts to jump. What your puppy needs to learn is that jumping makes the person go away, but keeping his feet on the floor makes the person approach. If the person actually reaches the puppy he or she should give the puppy lots of praise and petting. Practice this with a number of different people for the best results.

If jumping occurs when you have visitors come into your home, you should prevent this behavior as quickly as possible. One easy way to prevent jumping at the door is to crate your puppy before you answer the door. You can take him to his crate and give him a treat. Then let your visitors in and get settled. Once everyone is relaxed and seated then you can bring the puppy in on a leash. This makes the greeting a much calmer one.

Another method to teach your dog more appropriate behavior when visitors enter involves preventing the jumping by having your puppy on a leash and stepping on it about 1/3 of the way from the snap. You should allow enough room for your dog to sit and stand, but not to jump. Then you simply stand still on the leash and greet your guests. Don't scold your dog or try to make him sit, simply allow him to discover that he cannot jump on people. Again, this technique works well when you practice often with many different people. You can also use this method when you're out on a walk and someone approaches to greet you and your dog.

4. Chewing. All puppies, and many adult dogs, enjoy chewing. It is something that they physically need to do so it cannot (and should not) be eliminated. Dogs seem to find chewing a very satisfying pastime. Chewing serves an important purpose by allowing dogs to release pent-up energy and engage in a focused activity.

Chewing is only a problem when it is practiced on inappropriate objects (furniture, shoes, rugs, etc.) Puppies don't realize that there are inappropriate and appropriate chewing objects. To them, any object they encounter is fair game. Good management is important in keeping a puppy away from forbidden objects. Keeping things out of your puppy's reach will help to avoid destruction of valuable objects. I became a very neat housekeeper when my Golden Retriever (also known as 'Jaws' at the time) was a puppy. Closing bedroom doors and/or using baby gates can make a big difference. You should 'puppy proof' your house by crawling around on the floor (puppy height) and looking for possible temptations and dangers. For example, you should move your houseplants out of reach or into an area that will be off-limits to the puppy. Electrical cords can be quite dangerous if your puppy chews through them. You can either put up barricades to keep your puppy away from them, or invest in plastic cord covers. You may need to move your books and CD collection to higher shelves. By anticipating these types of problems, you can save yourself money and frustration later on.

Once you have completed your puppy-proofing, ideally BEFORE you bring your new puppy home, it's time to become proactive by providing a number of appropriate chew objects. The objects you provide must be both safe and appealing. Be sure that the chew objects you provide are strong enough to stand up to the most vigorous chewing. Large dogs with strong jaws (Labrador and Golden Retrievers, German Shepherds, Rottweilers, etc.) can destroy an object in minutes. Even smaller puppies can rip and shred their toys. However, there are literally thousands of dog

With a little care and forethought, you can find toys that are appropriate for your dog…

toys available, and with a little care and forethought, you can find toys that are appropriate for your dog.

In my opinion, the absolute best toy for any dog is a Kong™ toy. The Kong toy is made of a very strong rubber, yet it has enough 'give' to be satisfying for your dog to chew. Kong toys come in a number of sizes, from tiny to huge. A Kong toy is shaped in 3 tiers that resemble a beehive, an ice cream cone, or a snowman. Kong toys are hollow inside, and this is the key to their usefulness. While some dogs will enjoy chasing and chewing on the Kong toy, almost all dogs will enjoy having a 'stuffed' Kong.

Start by spreading a light layer of peanut butter or soft cheese around the inside of the Kong. Then add some dry kibble, shaking the Kong so that the kibble sticks to the peanut butter or cheese. Finally, wedge a biscuit in the opening. At first, you might also spread some peanut butter or cheese around the outside rim of the Kong, to entice your dog to start working on it. It takes some puppies a little longer than others to figure out how to 'unstuff' the Kong. Make it easy at first by packing the food and biscuits loosely, then harder later on once your pup gets the idea. Feed your puppy slightly less at his meals to compensate for the food he consumes from the Kong. You might also fill the Kong with a mixture of canned food and dry kibble, then freeze it. This seems to be very satisfying for puppies who are teething.

You can give your puppy a stuffed Kong any time you want him to be quiet and busy. These are especially useful when your puppy is crated and when you cannot keep an eye on him. As long as you decrease his regular food intake, you cannot overdo the use of a stuffed Kong. In fact, it is perfectly acceptable to feed your puppy nearly all his food in the Kong, rather than from a bowl.

You can also stuff sterilized bones (available at pet stores and through pet supply catalogs) for your puppy to chew. However, be very careful that the bones are hard and thick, and that your puppy cannot crack or splinter them.

There are a number of chew objects sold under the Nylabone brand name. Basic Nylabones are very tough and strong. They come in a variety of flavors (chicken, liver, etc.) and shapes (bones, rings, knots, etc.), and can be made even more enticing at first by spreading them with some peanut butter or cheese.

Many people give their dogs and puppies chew objects made of rawhide, as well as different animal parts (pig ears, cow hooves, etc.) I would caution you to be very, very careful when considering these objects. Personally, I never use them with my dogs. Some can cause intestinal upsets and others may crack or splinter with vigorous chewing. In addition, some dogs get quite possessive of these types of objects, and may growl or snap when you try to take them away.

Other types of toys might be appropriate for chase or tug games, but not for strong chewing. Fleece toys, squeaky toys, tug ropes and tennis balls can be safe and fun, but play should be closely supervised.

Whenever you find your dog chewing on an inappropriate object remove it and then replace it with an acceptable one. Don't punish your puppy excessively, this is not a major crime. Simply give him something that he is allowed to chew. Even better, be aware of your puppy's need for chewing, and have the appropriate objects readily available.

Puppies go through several strong chewing stages. The first occurs when they lose their baby teeth and get their adult ones. As you can imagine, this can be painful, and chewing can help ease the aching. Many dogs also go through a second chewing stage sometime between 9 months and 1 year of age. It has been suggested that this second stage is the result of changes in head size and shape, that again make the mouth and teeth ache. This second stage is the one that often catches owners by surprise. Just when they think that their puppy is maturing and getting easier to manage, they discover major damage from chewing. By being aware of this stage, you can be prepared.

If you understand your puppy's need to chew, and you are prepared to deal with it, you can get through puppyhood with a minimum of frustration and damage. Remember, don't punish your puppy for trying to satisfy this basic need. Instead, practice good environmental management (clean up your house!), supervise your puppy at all times, and provide safe and appropriate chew objects.

5. High activity levels. While some puppies are more active than others, they can all require more exercise and activity than most owners realize. In fact, I would be a bit concerned about the physical health of a very low energy puppy.

Again, it helps to be proactive and plan on satisfying your puppy's activity and exercise needs ahead of time. The schedule for housetraining listed earlier provides for daily walks, play time, and training time. By planning physical exercise such as play and walks, as well as mental exercise through training, you can avoid the problem of a bored, restless puppy. Our motto is "a tired puppy is a good puppy". You want to be careful, of course, not to overdo activity, but moderate physical and mental exercise can lead to a calmer, better behaved dog.

Physical activities can include games such as chase and fetch, as well as walking and running. It is very important to be careful not to overdo strenuous physical exercise, particularly for large breed puppies. Putting too much stress on growing joints and muscles can lead to lifelong problems. Physical exercise is safest on soft surfaces and should be carefully monitored. Allowing your puppy a chance to run free in an enclosed area and walking him on grass rather than concrete are usually safe exercises. Don't expect your puppy to be a jogging partner on long runs until he is an adult in good physical condition.

Fetch games can be a great way to exercise your puppy while keeping your time and energy investment to a minimum. Encourage your puppy to chase thrown or rolled objects, and to bring them back to you. Most dogs have a natural desire to retrieve, and will do so for a long period of time. Others need more coaching and encouragement.

If you leave your puppy alone for long hours while you work, you can expect him to be full of pent-up energy when you return home. First, make sure you give him some exercise and attention in the morning before you leave, even if you have to get up earlier than usual to do so. A quick walk, a bit of playtime, and a short training session will give your pup a chance to burn off some energy in the morning. Also, you'll need to make arrangements for someone to exercise your puppy at midday. Either a neighbor, friend, relative, or petsitter can help out if you cannot return home for a break. Your puppy needs a potty break, a treat or meal, and a bit of physical activity.

Most puppies have a 'crazy time' somewhere during the day. This is usually characterized by a quick burst of physical activity, such as running in circles. These times are actually called FRAPs (frantic random activity periods). These times are quick energy burners, and are usually quite amusing to watch as well! However, if the 'crazy time' includes jumping on people and nipping or biting, then your pup probably needs a short time-out.

Mental activity is just as important as physical activity. Short fun training sessions give your puppy's brain a chance to work. Puppies have very short attention spans, so don't expect him to be able to focus for very long at any given time. Make sure that your training sessions are always interesting and pleasant. This will give your dog a life long positive association with training.

KEY CONCEPT: Mental activity is just as important as physical activity.

A fun toy that will give your dog some mental exercise is called a Buster Cube™. The Buster Cube is a square hard plastic object that has a number of chambers inside. You place dry dog food into the center and shake it to distribute the food to all the chambers. In order to retrieve the food, your dog must manipulate the Buster Cube, usually by pawing, kicking, and nosing the cube. The food comes out randomly as the cube is manipulated. Some dogs get very vigorous in knocking the cube around, so do this in a safe place (an enclosed area outdoors is probably best). The purpose of the Buster Cube is to make the dog work for his food, rather than just letting him have it in a bowl. Along the same lines, you could simply scatter your puppy's food in the back yard (fenced, of course) and let him search and hunt for each kernel. This activity extends the mealtime and gives your puppy a chance to use his natural scenting ability to search out his food.

Exposing your puppy to new places and experiences is another way to exercise his mental muscles and to tire him out. Novel and unusual sights, sounds, and smells actually cause your puppy's brain to grow by making new connections between his brain cells. Make it your goal to expose your puppy to one new thing every day. You could take him with you while you run errands. You could take him to visit your next door neighbor. You could take him to the park to see ducks. You could introduce him to a brand new toy. There's a whole world of things that your puppy has never been exposed to, so it should be easy to provide him with a new experience every day.

III. Living With Humans 101 (a crash course in appropriate behavior)

Sometimes we get lucky and end up with a dog who is naturally easy to live with. He doesn't bark, chew, or jump. Everyone hopes to get one of these perfect pets. Most of the time, however, we need to work hard to teach our dogs how to live comfortably with humans. There are a few expectations that most of us have for our dogs and their behavior. If we work on these issues, we can co-exist peacefully and happily with our canine companions.

Staying Home Alone

Only a very few people can spend every minute of the day with their pets. Most of us must work, sometimes long hours, as well as having other obligations away from our homes. This means that our dogs must learn to be relaxed and comfortable while we are gone. Separation anxiety and destructiveness while the owner is absent are two widely reported behavior problems these days. The rise in the number of 'home alone' problems is probably the result of leaving dogs by themselves for longer and longer periods of time. Since dogs are very social creatures, being isolated can be a very unpleasant experience. However, with some forethought and consideration, your dog can be taught to tolerate being alone.

A puppy or an adult dog who is new to your household should be confined in some way. You can either use a crate or a confinement area blocked off by doors or baby gates. Leaving a puppy or new dog loose in your house without supervision is simply asking for trouble. It's not fair to the puppy or dog to give him too much freedom, then to get upset and punish him when he makes mistakes like having housetraining accidents or chewing on the furniture. Instead, prevent the problems

Leaving a puppy or new dog loose in your house without supervision is simply asking for trouble…

by keeping your dog in a safe confinement area.

Many owners choose crating, especially for puppies, to keep their dog safe and secure while they are gone. Some people object to crating, believing that it is mean and cruel to keep the dog confined. Most dogs, however, can learn to feel comfortable and secure in their crates. The key is to introduce crating properly by making the crate a pleasant place to be, and then giving the dog plenty of exercise and attention when he is not crated. Crates come in two basic types: a hard-sided plastic version and an open wire version. Crates also come in a wide variety of sizes. A crate for a puppy should not be too large. If it is, your puppy can go potty in one end and still lie down comfortably in the other. A properly sized puppy crate will not allow this extra room. If you want to buy a large crate that will fit your full-grown dog, simply block off one end with a wire partition and clips and enlarge it as your puppy grows. Your crate should be big enough for your dog to stand up, turn around, and lie down comfortably. You should always provide water for your crated dog. Indestructible metal water bowls are a good choice. It's a good idea to provide a mat, fleece pad, blanket, carpet square, or bed for your dog (as long as he doesn't chew it up).

The best way to introduce the crate to your dog is to simply set it up and take off the door or leave it open. Put your crate in a room you use often, such as your family room. Don't isolate your dog by crating him in the garage or basement. Keep his crate in a place where he is comfortable and spends lots of time. Feed your dog his meals in his crate. Don't close the door, just put his food dish in the crate and let him enter and leave as he wants. You can also toss treats into his crate and click when he enters to take them. As your dog becomes comfortable entering the crate you can close the door for a few seconds, click, give him a treat while he's still in the crate, then open the door and let him leave. Repeat often, extending the time he must wait in the crate before you click and treat. Treat this process as a game and your puppy will enjoy it as well.

Continue to extend the time that your puppy waits in the crate for his click and treat. You can also begin to leave the room momentarily while your puppy is crated, then return to click and treat. One important rule is to never, ever pay attention to your puppy if he is barking or whining in his crate. Follow the 'invisible dog' rule for this. A barking, whining dog does not exist. A quiet dog gets attention.

You can give your dog a stuffed Kong or bone while he is crated for a short period of time. Release him once he is finished. Make crating a quiet, normal event in your dog's life. Crate him for frequent short periods throughout the day. He will pick up on your attitude and become accustomed to being crated very quickly. Many dogs will voluntarily seek out their crates for a quick nap when they are tired.

You can follow the same advice as described for crating if you use a confinement space in your house. People often choose a porch, bathroom, or kitchen area as the dog's space. However, many times dogs still manage to be very destructive in small spaces and rooms. I've seen dogs who have peeled tile off the floors and gnawed through kitchen cabinet doors. Dogs will often remove baseboards. One client of mine had a Border Collie who managed to remove the entire door frame while she was gone at work. A confinement space must truly be dog-proofed in order to be safe.

When you first start leaving your dog alone try to do so for very short periods. Start with a quick trip next door or to the post office. Leave a radio or the television playing softly. Dim the lights a bit when you go. Don't make a big emotional scene on leaving or on returning. Crate the dog a few minutes before you leave and wait a few minutes on returning before you release him.

Many adult dogs are perfectly fine when left loose in the house. However, don't be too quick to leave your puppy free. If you think your dog is ready to be left loose, start with a restricted area and leave for a very short period of time. You can extend the time and space as long as your dog is not finding trouble. However, if he starts to have problems, go back to crating for a few more weeks, then try again.

Your dog may develop destructive behaviors during times of change or stress. Moving, a change in your schedule, or a change in those living in the home (human or animal) can all lead your dog to display unwanted behaviors. This may be a short-term problem, but it could become a bad habit if allowed to continue unchecked. Again, going back to confinement or crating for a few weeks will probably be helpful.

Some dogs, often those adopted as adults, display an overwhelming anxiety reaction when left alone. In severe cases of separation anxiety dogs can cause an incredible amount of damage, often to doors and windows in an attempt to escape. Crated dogs can become frantic and have been known to bend the bars of wire crates and even manage to pop open locked crate doors. In addition, dogs with separation anxiety usually have numerous housetraining accidents. Separation anxiety is an emotional, fear-based problem. You will probably need the help of a good trainer or behaviorist (using positive techniques, of course!) to successfully resolve separation anxiety issues.

Handling

In order to live comfortably with our dogs, and to properly care for them, we must be able to physically manipulate and handle them. It can be very difficult and traumatic to deal with a dog who is too shy or too aggressive to be touched. Dogs who live in close proximity to humans must be capable of accepting all sorts of physical interactions calmly. Veterinary check-ups and procedures, along with grooming and bathing, are the most common types of handling that a dog must learn to accept. In addition to regular petting, many dogs are pushed, pulled or prodded at one time or another (particularly by children). Dogs who react poorly to routine handling or those who are 'touchy' or 'sensitive' can be difficult to live with.

As always, it is easiest to teach your dog to tolerate handling if you start when he is very young. However, it is never too late. Even older dogs can learn to accept routine handling in a calm and relaxed manner. Puppies should be gently stroked all over their bodies daily. With each stroke you can click and give a tasty treat. Your handling should also include the types of interactions your puppy/dog will have at the vet's office or groomers.

'Play doctor' with your pup by simulating the handling he will receive during a vet visit. Your vet will look at your dog's teeth, examine his ears and eyes, feel his chest and midsection (listen to his heartbeat), check the motion in his legs by manipulating them, even look under his tail (possibly take his temperature). All of these actions should be practiced in a relaxed setting (OK maybe not the temperature part!) If your dog has a 'touchy' area, proceed slowly, giving lots of clicks and treats when your dog relaxes. A groomer will brush and bathe your dog, clean out ears, cut toenails, use scissors and/or clippers on your dog's coat, and may use a loud, powerful blow dryer on your dog. Groomers usually place dogs on grooming tables and restrain them with a neck loop (called a noose) for these procedures.

It is easiest to practice handling when your dog is relaxed, calm, even tired. After the evening walk would be an excellent time to accustom your dog to being handled and manipulated. Many people practice basic massage techniques on their dogs, and most dogs love this.

Daily handling can alert you to any physical problems your dog might be developing. A dog who suddenly becomes touchy or sensitive in a particular area needs to be checked out by your vet. Also, a lump or bump (even a small one) might indicate the possibility of a health problem and should be evaluated by your veterinarian.

An important part of handling your dog is being able to take hold of his collar. Some dogs have learned to try to avoid having their collars touched or held. Often, owners have taken the collar in anger or when punishing the dog, so this type of handling is seen as a bad thing by the dog. Many times, the owner takes the collar and attaches the leash when play time is over. Your dog may try to avoid

having the fun end by avoiding being held by the collar.

A client of mine was bitten by a friend's twelve-year-old dog as she was petting him. She had accidentally touched his collar, and he bit. The (now former) friend later said "oh, he doesn't like to have his collar touched." My client ended up with a nasty bite and a trip to the emergency room because this dog had never become accustomed to routine handling.

Start collar handling and touching very gently. Reach towards your dog's collar with your left hand while, at the same time, giving him a treat with your right hand. Touch the collar very lightly while your dog eats the treat, praising quietly. As your dog accepts this process, proceed to actually taking hold of the collar while you feed your dog a treat from the other hand. Continue to handle the collar by lightly twisting and shaking it while your dog eats his treat. Our goal is to teach the dog that it's a very good thing when someone takes hold of his collar. You might call your dog, take his collar, give him a treat, then release him again to "go play". Progress to taking the collar and attaching a leash, then give a treat, and remove the leash. Your dog should learn to accept this fairly quickly.

With a small dog it can be very important to pick him up quickly. Larger dogs may suddenly approach in a menacing manner. A group of excited and rowdy children may converge on him suddenly. You may find yourself in the middle of a fast moving crowd on the sidewalk. It's worth the effort to teach your dog to accept, and even to enjoy, being picked up.

If you have a smaller dog, you will want to teach him to allow you to pick him up without having to chase him down and corner him. Sometimes small dogs try to avoid being picked up because it hurts. Be sure to pick up your small dog carefully, supporting both ends. If your dog yips, yelps, or nips when picked up, have your vet check him for possible physical problems. Back problems, in particular, can cause pain on being picked up.

Once you've ruled out any physical problems you can teach your little dog to calmly accept being picked up and held. Start by encouraging your dog to approach you while you sit on the floor. Feed him treats when he comes close. Reach for him but don't pick him up. Instead, give him a goodie and let him go. You need to teach him that he can choose to approach you and that you won't scoop him up against his will. Progress to picking him up one inch off the floor, popping a treat in his mouth while you hold him, and putting him down immediately. It's important to give the treat as you are holding him. You may need another person to help with this if you're not very coordinated. When your dog will willingly approach you and let you pick him up briefly, move to being on your knees and picking him up just a bit higher. Continue to pop in the treat and then put him down immediately. Next you can move to sitting on the couch or a chair, repeating the pick up, give a treat, put down, sequence. If your dog is doing well at this point you can add a verbal cue such as "with me" or "get close" or "up" right before

Start by encouraging your dog to approach while sitting on the floor...

you pick up your dog. Move to standing upright while enticing your dog to approach you, then briefly picking him up, giving him a treat, and releasing him. Sometimes, entice your dog to come close and give him the treat without picking him up. This encourages him to eagerly come to you.

If your dog struggles once you pick him up, hold very still and wait until he stops struggling before you put him down. A client of mine once had a really cute mini-Dachshund who would flip and flop once she was in your arms. It was like trying to hold a snake! Don't reward struggling by releasing your dog. For safety with a dog like this, hook your thumb through the collar so you won't drop him. Instead of releasing him when he struggles, go back to a quick pick up and put down, only giving a treat when the dog holds still while in your arms.

Kids & Dogs

Even if you don't have children in your home, your dog will probably have some interaction with them when out in public. Children do unexpected and sometimes downright stupid things to dogs. They pull, poke, prod, and grab. Rule number one concerning dogs and children is to never, ever leave them alone together, not even well-behaved dogs and children. Many incidents occur because a dog and child were unsupervised, and you'll never know for sure what actually occurred. A few years ago a client called who had left her 3-year-old son alone with their 5-month-old Labrador puppy. She heard a scream and returned to find her son's ear torn open and bleeding. He required twelve stitches and now has a fear of dogs. We had no way of knowing if the bite was provoked or not. In any case, this incident should not have occurred.

Many children have never been taught that dogs are living creatures who feel pain. As a responsible owner, it's up to you to protect your dog in these situations. However, it can be helpful to accustom your dog to the types of handling he might encounter from children so that it isn't too upsetting when it happens.

My Labrador Retriever, Katie, has worked as a pet therapist for many years. We've visited schools, children's hospitals, hospices, and nursing homes. Katie has had to learn to calmly accept all kinds of poking and prodding. She has had her tail stepped on, had her foot run over by a wheelchair, and been given a 'death grip' by one patient who refused to let go. She's even had her toenails polished by my daughter and granddaughter! Clearly, it takes a dog with a calm and steady personality to withstand these experiences. However, it also helps to have prepared a dog for these possibilities ahead of time. Obviously, we're not going to actually hurt the dog, but we can simulate some of the experiences.

Children run, scream, trip, fall, and grab. If you have a child around who is old enough to follow directions and is willing to help, you can ask her to perform some of these behaviors in a controlled setting and manner. Have the child run past your dog while laughing or yelling. When this occurs, click and treat your dog for remaining calm. If your dog gets too excited, have the child tone down her behavior and move a bit further away. Progress to having the child run toward your dog, but stop about 10 feet away. Again, click and treat if your dog remains calm. If your dog gets too excited, have the child stop at twice the distance. Then have the child approach your dog to give him a treat (held in the flat of her palm) while you click. Ask the child to pet your dog gently, then a bit more vigorously. Always try to click and treat before your dog gets too excited or upset.

You can also accustom your dog to rougher handling yourself. Start by petting gently, then become more forceful and vigorous in your massaging. Pull very lightly on your dog's ears. Squeeze his feet slightly. Tug his tail just a bit. Give him playful little shoves and pushes. Give him a big bear hug. Wrap your arms around his midsection and give a slight squeeze. Do all this with a happy, fun attitude and praise him for accepting it. Obviously, you don't want to hurt your dog, but you do want him to take a bit of unexpectedly rough handling in stride.

Good Manners

Often, pet owners don't expect a lot from their dogs, just good manners. However, good manners can mean different things to different people. In general, dogs are usually expected to follow a few simple rules. First, our dogs should not hurt us through rough physical interaction (jumping, bumping, bouncing, nipping, etc.). Second, our dogs should not steal our possessions, particularly our food. Third, when we request a behavior that our dogs know and understand, they should comply. Let's take a closer look at how to attain each of these expectations.

KEY CONCEPT: Our dogs should not hurt us through rough physical interaction, should not steal our possessions, and should comply when we request a behavior they know and understand.

We need to teach our dogs to control their physical interactions with humans. Most dogs have the capacity to hurt human beings. Even if they don't use their teeth, dogs can knock people down and scratch or bruise them.

Even though I'm fairly careful of my personal safety I've had a number of incidents occur. I once tripped over a dog and sprained my wrist (that one wasn't the dog's fault!) I've also been knocked into walls by obnoxious out-of-control Labrador Retrievers (we call them "bumper dogs" for good reason). My nose was broken by a Border Collie/Australian Shepherd mix who jumped up to my face height and head-butted me before I could blink an eye. As I reached for a Golden Retriever's collar my finger caught it wrong and a tendon snapped. A Cairn Terrier puppy took exception when I tried to hold him and nearly severed an artery in my wrist. Of course, I often work with 'problem' dogs, but dog-related physical accidents are not uncommon.

To begin teaching your dog to be careful around humans, don't allow bad habits to start. Many owners don't think about the fact that the cute little puppy who is trying to leap into their arms will soon be an uncontrollable 60 pound dog. The best rule to follow is to never allow a puppy to do something you don't want him to do as an adult. It isn't fair to let him get into bad habits, then to punish him later on for those same behaviors. If you have a puppy who is expected to grow into a large, strong dog, keep that image in mind throughout puppyhood. If you have a toy-sized dog who will never get very large you don't have the same concerns as owners of larger dogs. However, even small dogs can inflict painful bites, can scratch, and can get underfoot to trip humans.

An important lesson for dogs to learn is that it is their job to get out of the way of humans. I give this behavior the verbal cue of "move". "Move" means that I am coming through and you (the dog) need to give way so I don't trip over you. If I'm carrying something, like groceries, I may not be able to see the ground. If the path before me is blocked it may not be safe to step over the dog. A person who has physical mobility problems may not be able to maneuver around the dog lying in front of him. In any case, I simply would like the dog to get out of my way so I can continue through.

Most dogs will step aside and yield space as people step towards them. It's not wise or necessary to physically step on the dog, but simply move into his space in a slow and deliberate manner. As you move towards the dog and he gives way (even slightly), click and toss a treat in the direction he was moving. This encourages him to continue moving out of your path. While you can add the verbal cue of "move" to this behavior, It's nice if your dog develops an automatic "moving" response to you moving into his space. Rather than having to give the cue, I'd simply like for the dog to move away as I move towards him. Simply clicking and treating (making sure to toss the treat further away from you) will do the trick here.

Teaching your dog to 'wait' is another way to control his physical interactions with people. Instead of a formal sit or down 'stay', this is a very short, informal 'wait'. The wait can occur with your dog in any position (sit, down, or stand). It simply means to your dog "hold still for a few seconds". To begin training this behavior, encourage your dog to hold still next to you for a moment. You can use a hand signal here, placing your open flat palm right in front of your dog's nose. If your dog hesitates,

even for a second, click and treat. Slowly extend the time you wait before you click and treat (by seconds). Once your dog is regularly stopping and waiting when you give the hand signal, add the verbal cue to "wait" right before you give the hand signal. The sequence will become: verbal cue to "wait", hand signal, short pause, click, treat. Practice this sequence at different times with your dog in a sit, down, and stand. Stay right next to or in front of your dog until he is holding still for about 20 seconds.

Once your dog has a steady wait, you can start moving slightly away from him. Remind him to wait with both your verbal cue and hand signal. Take a short step away, return immediately, click and treat. You want to leave and return fairly quickly, without your dog moving from position. If your dog is moving when you move, remind him to wait in a calm and quiet voice, and simply bend your body slightly (as if moving). Reinforce him with a click and treat for being still. As your dog comes to understand the wait exercise you can move further and further away, clicking and treating only when your dog is actually holding still.

Here are a couple of scenarios in which a wait would be useful. You are trying to open your front door and are juggling keys and a grocery bag while holding your dog's leash. Ask him to sit and wait while you open the door, then release him to go inside. Or, you are walking your dog through a crowd at an oudoor art show. You want to stop to look at some merchandise and you simply tell your dog to wait while you move a few steps away to examine the goods. Then you release him when you're ready to move on. Or, you have just returned home from a walk with your dog and his paws are muddy. Stop him at the door and tell him to wait while you grab a towel to wipe his paws.

Some dogs seem to spend very little time with all four feet on the ground. They bounce and jump quite often and with great enthusiasm. Maybe they're part kangaroo?! We need to teach them to keep their feet on the ground, especially when interacting with people. If you play with your dog and allow him to wrestle and jump, it will be harder to teach him not to interact with others in the same way. Most dogs find it difficult to understand why certain behaviors are okay in one situation or with one person, but not in other situations or with other people. Check out the suggestions under the Puppy Problems section for dealing with jumping problems.

Some dogs have trouble distinguishing between stuff that belongs to them and stuff that belongs to you. Some of this is the owner's fault as we haven't been clear about what's off limits to our dogs (by leaving it within doggie reach). Some of this may have a genetic basis, certain dogs are naturally more possessive and protective of objects than others. In some cases, it may be that only certain objects elicit possessiveness (such as bones or rawhides). Again, good management is the key to avoiding problems before they start. Keep your treasured objects out of the dog's reach. Keep the doors to the kids' rooms closed.

Some dogs seem to spend very little time with all four feet on the ground...

One technique that has been reported to help dogs distinguish between their toys and the kids' toys is to mark the kids' toys with a small dab of Listerine mouthwash. The mouthwash will smell and taste unpleasant to the dog and he will avoid it. However, once the Listerine dries the kids won't notice it. You can reapply the Listerine every few days if necessary.

It is fairly easy to teach your dog to move away from or give up objects that you don't want him to have. The exercises we teach for these situations are 'leave it!', 'give me that!' and 'trade?'. Each of these exercises can be taught in a pleasant and positive manner, so that your dog will want to avoid taboo objects or give back inappropriate ones.

LEAVE IT!

The purpose of the 'leave it!' cue is to teach your dog to turn away from forbidden objects and to come back to you. The world is full of things that could be dangerous for your dog. Chicken bones are left on the sidewalk. Antifreeze leaks onto driveways. Unfriendly dogs are walked by their owners. For your dog's safety, you need to teach him to avoid certain things when necessary.

It is very unpleasant and ineffective to pull your dog away from objects and yell at him. Instead, we want the dog to willingly turn away from objects and to happily return to us. Begin teaching 'leave it!' by setting up a mild distraction for your dog. We have a helper who either has a toy or some dry dog kibble. The helper's job is to gain the dog's attention, then completely ignore him. The owner will then lure the dog away with a very desirable treat. When the dog turns away from the distraction the owner clicks and continues luring the dog by taking a few steps backward before giving the treat. Our target behavior is the dog turning away from the distraction and moving toward the owner. When the dog turns away from the distraction every time the owner moves in with the lure then the lure can be faded out and the owner can simply use a luring hand motion. Click and treat after the dog follows the hand motion and moves away from the distraction. Finally, the verbal cue 'leave it!' (said in a very pleasant voice) can be added right before the luring hand motion. Allow a slight pause (several seconds) between the verbal cue and the hand

motion. Soon you should see your dog respond to the verbal cue alone.

Steps to teach 'leave it!':
1. Have a helper gain your dog's attention with a mild distraction.
2. Instruct the helper to completely ignore your dog once the dog focuses on the helper.
3. When the dog is distracted move towards him and lure him away with a treat.
4. When the dog is regularly responding to the lure fade it out and use a luring hand motion without the treat. Click and treat after the dog moves away from the distraction and towards you.
5. When the dog is regularly responding to the luring hand motion add the verbal cue "leave it!" (said in a pleasant voice) right before the hand motion. Click and treat after the dog moves away from the distraction and towards you.
6. Allow a slight pause between the verbal cue and your luring hand motion. Your dog should begin to respond to the verbal cue alone.

Once your dog has a basic understanding of 'leave it!' you can increase the level of distraction. Gradually make the distractions more and more difficult for your dog to ignore. Have your helper hold one of your dog's favorite toys or use better treats to entice him. Remind the helper to completely ignore the dog once he has his attention. The dog should NEVER actually get the treats or toys that the helper has. Your dog is learning that all good things come from you. When you increase the level of the distractions you should also increase the value of your reinforcer.

Once your dog is able to leave objects in a controlled training setting, it's time to use "leave it!" on real life distractions. You can use anything that your dog wants to go toward as a distraction. Instead of being annoyed when your dog pulls toward or wants to investigate things he cannot have, consider it a training opportunity. Imagine that your dog would like to investigate a pizza box that someone carelessly left on the sidewalk. As you see your dog's interest in the object; stop and hold still. Start moving backwards and verbally cue your dog to "leave it!". If you've done your groundwork on this exercise, your dog will turn and move towards you. Click and/or use a verbal secondary reinforcer. Give him a treat, or a whole handful of treats if the distraction was a difficult one to ignore. Then take a wide detour around the pizza box as you continue on your way.

GIVE ME THAT!

I first learned about the 'give me that!' exercise from a trainer named Sue Sternberg who works extensively with shelter dogs. Her goal is to teach these dogs enough in the way of basic manners to make them good companions for their new owners. In considering the possible situations dogs may encounter in their new homes, she came up with a great way to teach dogs to release objects we don't want them to have. To begin, walk up to your dog when he isn't paying any attention to you, say "give me that!", and pop a treat in his mouth. Do this in all types of settings at various times. You

are teaching your dog that when he hears the phrase "give me that!" he should open his mouth so you can give him a treat. This behavior will carry over to times when your dog has an object you want him to drop. Simply tell him "give me that!". He will open his mouth in anticipation of his treat and drop the object. Pick up the object he drops, praise him lavishly, and go get him a treat. This is a much easier and gentler method than chasing him down and trying to wrestle objects out of his mouth.

TRADE?

Another method that I developed to get a dog to give up something he already has is "trade?". I started using this exercise when my Golden Retriever was a puppy. He ALWAYS had something he shouldn't, no matter how good I was about management. I decided that I wanted to teach him to bring me the things he would inevitably pick up, then I could praise him for giving them to me rather than yell at him for picking them up in the first place. The basic concept is that the dog can 'trade' his treasures for a treat.

Start teaching trade when your dog has a forbidden object (as long as the object isn't dangerous). With dangerous objects practice much better environmental management and do whatever it takes to keep your dog safe. With things like shoes, pillows, books, etc. you can practice the trade exercise. When your dog has a forbidden object show him a really good, smelly treat. If possible, hold the treat right in front of his nose. Don't make any effort to take the object from his mouth, just wait. Most dogs will be a bit conflicted at first, but eventually decide to drop the object to take the treat. When this happens use your verbal secondary reinforcer "Yes!"or "Great!" while the dog eats the treat, and pick up the dropped object with your other hand. Now comes the key part of this exercise — GIVE THE OBJECT BACK TO YOUR DOG (unless It's something dangerous). Now you can repeat the exercise. Your dog is learning that he can give up his treasures, get something even better from you, then get the treasure back. This makes him much less likely to resist giving things up. You can use the verbal cue "trade?" right before you place the treat on your dog's nose.

In our training classes we begin teaching "trade?" by having the dog on a leash and standing on the leash so he cannot try to run away and hide with his object. As with the "leave it!" exercise, we start with a low value trade object and gradually increase the value. For example, it may be next to impossible to get your Labrador Retriever to give up his tennis ball, but much easier to get him to give up a fleece toy.

Steps to teach "trade?"
  1. Have your dog on leash and stand on it, leaving enough slack for him to move around, but keeping him in your general vicinity.
  2. Give your dog an object of relatively low value (remember, value is determined by each individual dog).
  3. When your dog takes the object in his mouth put a very desirable treat on his nose and wait.
  4. When your dog drops the object to take the treat use your secondary verbal reinforcer and give him the treat.
  5. With your other hand pick up the dropped object.
  6. Give the dropped object back to your dog and repeat the exercise.
  7. When your dog starts dropping the object when you move the treat toward his nose add the "trade?" verbal cue right before you move the treat toward him.
  8. Start allowing a short delay (3-5 seconds) between the verbal cue and the presentation of the treat. Your dog will soon start responding to the verbal cue.

You might think that your dog will figure out that he should bring you stuff whenever he wants a goodie. In fact, the smarter dogs will figure this out. When the dog reaches this point we stop giving treats for a while and simply praise for giving up the object. At that point most dogs don't see the point in the whole process and they stop picking up everything they encounter.

What we've done is teach our dogs that the objects they find are not as valuable as the treats they can earn on trade-in. The dog becomes focused on the treat rather than on possessing the object. When we stop giving so many treats most dogs lose interest in the objects as well. Once again, we've been smarter than our dogs, not faster or stronger. We get what we want by using brain power, not muscle.

Food possessiveness

Many possessiveness problems develop over food. Some dogs seem to be much more protective of their food than others. This tendency to guard food can escalate over time and end up with aggressive reactions such as growling, snapping, and biting. It is important to avoid eliciting these types of responses and to teach the dog appropriate ways to behave around food.

First, it is a good idea to feed your dog from your hand sometimes rather than from a bowl. By feeding your dog one piece of kibble at a time you are teaching him that you control the food delivery. You are also helping him to make a positive association, rather than a negative one, between human hands and food. When you do feed from a bowl sit on the floor next to your dog and put the food in a few pieces at a time as he eats it. He'll look forward to your hands in his bowl as that means more food is coming. If you start this with your new puppy he will probably never develop food possessiveness.

If your dog already has 'issues' with food you will need to be more careful in your approach to this problem. Don't push your dog (being too close, having your hands in his bowl) until he feels threatened by your presence. He may snap in response. Work through this problem slowly, never increasing your demands until your dog is comfortable at each step. Be especially careful of children around a dog who is food possessive. Don't allow them to

Teach your dogs that the objects they find are not as valuable as the treats they can earn on a trade-in...

be in a position where the dog may perceive them as a threat.

Your dog deserves a chance to eat in a quiet, peaceful environment. While he doesn't need absolute privacy, he should be able to take his time and be relaxed while eating. Dogs become possessive and protective when they feel that their food will be taken from them. Imagine how you would feel if someone hovered over you during your meals, constantly grabbing at your plate and your food. If you come from a large family this may have actually happened to you! You can avoid creating problems by feeding the dog in a quiet place and keeping activity to a minimum during feeding time. People can certainly be present, but should be fairly calm and quiet while the dog is actually eating.

COMPLIANCE

It is essential that we train our dogs to do what we ask. A compliant dog is eager and ready to respond to our requests. I'm not talking about military style orders and precise responses here, but basic reasonable requests that we expect to be obeyed. I want my dogs to respond in a willing and enthusiastic manner; not out of fear or due to coercion and force.

In order to gain voluntary compliance, we need to build up a reinforcement history with our dogs. The term reinforcement history refers to a pattern of interaction that is established between dog and owner. In this interaction the owner makes appropriate requests and demands that the dog is able to successfully perform. The dog is then reinforced for that performance. The dog comes to learn that good things happen when you comply with your owner's requests. It is in the dog's best interest to comply.

You can use anything that your dog needs or wants as reinforcement for compliance. The use of Life Rewards, described in Chapter 3, can be a good way to gain compliance. For example, if your dog wants to go outside you can ask him to sit before you open the door. The sooner he sits, the sooner you open the door to let him out. You control your dog's access to the things he wants. Once your dog understands that you control everything he wants, compliance will be easy to obtain. Make it clearly to your dog's advantage to do the things you want.

It is important to have realistic and reasonable expectations regarding your dog's behavior. Dogs are not little furry robots. They are living breathing creatures. They make mistakes sometimes. They forget their manners. They are tempted to misbehave when the opportunity presents itself. Nobody's perfect, either canine or human. Rather than blame our dogs for acting like dogs, we need to work on our training and management to help us avoid or deal with problems that may arise.

Even though we may be understanding of our dogs' limitations, there are certain safety issues for which compliance is vital. We've already considered cases where dogs might hurt humans. There are also situations in which dogs may harm themselves if they don't respond to us immediately and appropriately. Teaching your dog to come when called is probably the most important of all obedience exercises for your dog's well-being and safety. By constantly reinforcing your dog for coming when called, and training in steps designed to lead to success along the way, your dog can learn a very reliable recall (more on this in Chapter 6).

So what should you do if your dog doesn't comply with a command? That depends on a number of factors. First, are you absolutely positive that your dog truly understands what you are requesting? Has he reliably complied with the request in the past? Second, is there something in the environment that is leading to a lack of compliance? Is the dog overly stressed, distracted, or nervous? If the environment is too overwhelming your dog may be incapable of responding appropriately without further training. Lack of compliance is rarely intentional on the dog's part. Our dogs do not lay around thinking "the next time she asks me to sit I'm going to ignore her".

In general, if your dog does not comply with a command, it is due to a training deficiency or an overwhelming distraction. Dogs do whatever is most rewarding at any given time. Your job is to lay a solid training foundation so that your dog finds compliance to be the most rewarding thing he can do. Don't blame the dog, train the dog. Good dog trainers know that it is nearly always the trainer's fault when the dog's performance is poor.

IV. Pleased to Meet Ya! (Socialization)

Socialization is a term that refers to providing your puppy with early exposure to people, other dogs, and other animals. It is important to provide a wide variety of safe experiences early in your puppy's life. These early experiences will lead to a dog who is calm and relaxed around unfamiliar people and animals. When a dog is not socialized early in life, he may become fearful, suspicious, and even aggressive.

It has long been believed that there is a critical period in which the puppy must be socialized. The critical period is a window of opportunity; a time in which it will be easiest to learn certain things. Once that window of opportunity closes, it will be much more difficult, or even impossible, for specific types of learning to occur. In this case we are talking about learning that people and other animals are safe and friendly.

It has long been accepted that, ideally, a puppy needs to be socialized between 7 and 16 weeks of age. Unfortunately, this critical period comes in direct conflict with the advice of many veterinarians who have said that a puppy's exposure to the outside world should be limited in that same time frame for health reasons. Many veterinarians suggest that a puppy needs to have finished his series of immunizations (around 16 weeks old) prior to exposure to others. However, some vets are now amending these recommendations. It has become obvious that the life-long consequences of a lack of socialization are more problematic than the small possibility of exposure to an infectious disease. The decision about when to begin socialization needs to be made with an educated understanding of both behavioral and health issues.

Whenever you decide to begin socializing your puppy, do it slowly and carefully. Choose situations in which your puppy will be safe and will feel secure. Make sure other dogs are friendly, healthy, and fully immunized. Make sure the humans understand that the puppy needs calm and gentle handling. These early experiences will have a major impact on your puppy, so you want them to be as positive as possible. Don't overwhelm your pup at first. Introduce him to the world slowly and carefully. Avoid situations where you cannot control the environment. For example, public off-leash dog parks and pet superstores should be avoided. You don't know whether the other dogs are friendly or if they are healthy. You wouldn't necessarily be able to protect your puppy should an altercation occur. Instead, find a friend who has a nice, well-trained adult dog. Introduce the dogs in a quiet environment and keep their interactions short and controlled at first.

Make sure that your puppy has the opportunity to meet all kinds of people. Without exposure, some dogs develop fears of men, children, people with hats, etc. Try to expose your pup to a wide variety of people. Ask them to talk to him quietly and offer him a tasty treat. If he seems a bit shy don't push things. Let him hang back, observe, and move forward at his own pace. Some puppies are social butterflies and love everyone while others are a bit more cautious about meeting strangers. Give the cautious ones plenty of opportunities for relaxed interactions, but don't force them to directly interact with other people or animals until they are ready. Once you've started clicker training you can click and treat during interactions. Click and treat your puppy for showing any interest in strangers. Whenever he voluntarily approaches someone, click and treat. Soon he'll become braver and more confident.

If your puppy is fearful, resist the desire to comfort and stroke him. If you do this, you are actually reinforcing the fearful behavior and it will increase. Instead, be very calm and relaxed. Give your puppy the chance to work out his fears on his own. Let him hide behind you if he really needs to, but ignore him when he does. Pay attention to his brave behaviors, not his fearful ones.

If your puppy becomes overly excited by interactions, move him slightly away from the person or animal and give him a short break. Puppies are like children and they can get too 'cranked up' to behave properly. A puppy in this state might lunge, jump, nip, bark, or whine. When this happens he needs a short time-out so that he can regain his composure. Interactions with others should only be allowed when the puppy is relatively calm and in control.

In addition to exposing your puppy to people and other animals, you also want to expose him to a variety of situations. Riding in a car, walking in the park, hearing and seeing traffic, and watching crowds are just a few examples of the experiences your dog should have while he is relatively young. With early exposure, keep the time short and stay at a distance. For example, you might take your pup on a trip to the park. Imagine that there is a soccer game going on. Keep plenty of distance and just give your pup a chance to see and hear the activity. The next trip you might move a bit closer and stay a little longer. Gradual exposure will allow your puppy a chance to get used to new situations while remaining calm and relaxed.

Many puppies will go through a fear period at some point in their early development. A fear period is a time when the pup seems to be extremely sensitive to experiences and may perceive them as threatening or frightening. This can happen even when the puppy seems to have a fairly bold and confident personality. Many times, the fear period appears and then disappears rapidly. However, if your puppy seems to develop some lingering fearful tendencies, you will need to work slowly and carefully to show him that the world really is a safe place.

Don't let socialization be a 'hit or miss' experience. Plan your puppy's introduction to the world with care. Give him the opportunity to learn that the world, and the creatures in it, are fun, interesting, and safe.

KEY CONCEPTS REVISITED:

Puppies are always learning. It's up to each to teach them the things we want them to know. Learning occurs constantly. It is not something that only happens during training sessions. Life is one long training session for your puppy! Take advantage of that and train your puppy to behave appropriately with every interaction.

Mental activity is just as important as physical activity. The brain grows and develops just as the body does. Puppies need to have all their senses stimulated through new experiences. They need to keep their minds, as well as their bodies, active.

Our dogs should not hurt us through rough physical interaction, should not steal our possessions, and should comply when we request a behavior they know and understand. However, the key to getting these things is through management and positive training, not through force. We need to teach our dogs how we want them to behave and prevent them from behaving in unacceptable ways.

For further reading/viewing:
Taking Care of Puppy Business *by Leslie Nelson*
Clicker Training for Puppies (video) *by Karen Pryor*

Genetics and the Social Behavior of the Dog: The Classic Study *by John Paul Scott and John L. Fuller*

Our dogs do not lay around thinking "the next time she asks me to sit I'm going to ignore her"...

Chapter 6

Fido Don't Know Sit

— But He Can Learn! —

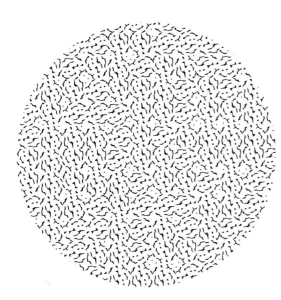

It is unfair to expect our dogs to behave 'properly' unless we have put the time and effort into teaching them how we want them to act. Sure, once in a while you get lucky, and you find a dog who very rarely gets into trouble. That is unusual, though, and you shouldn't expect that all dogs will simply pick up what they need to know without any effort on your part. If you are taking on the responsibility of a canine companion, you are now also responsible for his education. The good news is that, using clicker training, it is possible to train your dog to be a good canine citizen in a fun and enjoyable way.

We often joke in obedience classes that most dogs "don't know sit". In fact, they often don't understand the verbal cue if it is presented without repetition, body language, and increased volume. However, owners truly believe that their dogs do understand the cue to "sit". To test this understanding in your dog stand up perfectly straight, keep your voice neutral, and keep your hands behind your back or in your pockets when you ask your dog to sit. Now, does he truly understand? Does he respond quickly and confidently on the first cue? If not, a bit more foundation work is in order.

Finding Instruction

For most people, the best way to learn and practice basic obedience exercises is in a class setting with hands-on instruction. Dog obedience instructors are available in most areas of the world. Finding the right one is crucial to your success with clicker training.

The 'Resources' section will give you some leads to finding a clicker trainer in your area. However, you may have to do your own searching. Call local trainers and ask about their training methods and techniques. Ask if you can observe a class before you register. Avoid trainers who still use force-based techniques, or who try to mix forceful methods with positive reinforcement and clicker training. These trainers clearly do not understand learning theory and will not maintain a positive approach. It is better to travel some distance to find the right trainer than to take a class where punishment-based techniques are advocated.

It is possible, but more difficult, to train without the help of an instructor. If necessary, you can design your own training plan using information from clicker books and videos. Possibly, you may be able to attend a weekend seminar or two on clicker training to give you some in-person experience.

KEY CONCEPT: *It is better to find a trainer who truly endorses the concepts of clicker training and positive reinforcement than to take a traditional, force-based training class.*

I. Equipment

To begin clicker training you will need to have the proper equipment readily available. First, of course, you need a clicker. Actually, you will probably find it most convenient to have several clickers. Since they are small it is very easy to misplace them. On rare occasions, a clicker will break. Over time, the click becomes softer and softer. Since they are cheap, keep plenty of clickers on hand. The 'Resources' section contains information on where to obtain clickers.

Next you will need to obtain a variety of desirable treats. The treats need to be soft, small, and easy for your dog to swallow. Experiment with treats to find what works best for your dog. Also, providing variety in treats helps to maintain your dog's interest.

You will need a place to store your treats during training. Some trainers simply keep the treats in a pocket. However, you want quick access to your treats, so you might find it cumbersome to keep digging into your pockets. Many trainers have found that a carpenter's apron or fanny pack gives them a convenient place to keep treats and clickers readily available.

Many people find that certain toys work well as reinforcers. If you decide to use desirable toys as training tools, keep them only for training, not for general play. A tuggy toy is a good choice as it can be used for a quick game, then taken away until the next reinforcement.

A collar and leash are often required while training, particularly in a group class or public place. If you are training at home in a secure environment, they are probably not necessary. For most dogs a plain buckle or quick release snap collar and a 6 foot leash (leather or nylon) are the best choices. Another good choice for a collar is a martingale. The martingale keeps a dog from slipping his head out of the collar by tightening just a limited amount. Dog who have sleek, small heads such as Greyhounds and Doberman Pinschers often benefit from these collars. The martingale also offers slightly more control than a buckle collar.

For a very strong, energetic dog, or a dog who needs even more control in certain situations, a head halter might be necessary. Head halters have both a nose loop and a neck loop. A head halter can be a good training tool and, once training has taken place, the use of the head halter can be phased out. It is important to have a qualified trainer instruct you in the proper fit and gradual introduction of a head halter. If you simply slap the head halter on a dog without taking the time to accustom him to the feel of it, he is very likely to resist. However, introducing the head halter by pairing it with treats, and allowing the dog plenty of time to get used to the feel of the nose loop, can lead the dog to accept it readily. Most dogs have never felt anything on their muzzles before, and it can feel strange and uncomfortable at first. By allowing your dog to repeatedly go through the process of putting on the nose loop, getting a treat, then taking off the nose loop, he will relax and realize that it's no big deal. In addition to proper fit and initial training, it is important to follow all directions for using the head halter safely. In particular, it is vital to avoid any jerking or sharp tugs on the leash when a head halter is being used.

Due to the likelihood of misuse and their ability to cause tracheal damage, choke or slip collars are not recommended. These collars put an enormous amount of pressure on a very sensitive part of the dog's throat. Some dogs react to this pressure by choking, gasping, or wheezing. Even if these outward signs of distress are not present, these collars can cause internal damage. Pinch or prong collars are also not recommended. They work because they inflict pain. These types of collars are especially dangerous on dogs who have aggressive tendencies. Adding physical pain to an already emotionally aroused animal is very likely to lead to increased aggression.

Be sure to have the correct equipment available, and become familiar with the proper and safe use of that equipment, before you start training.

II. Cues & Signals

Stimulus Control

The term stimulus control is used to describe the ability of an external stimulus (cue or signal) to control the performance of a behavior. If you say "stop!" and your child freezes in his tracks, you have stimulus control. If you say "sit" and your dog's rear end hits the floor, you have stimulus control. If you say "come here" and your dog sniffs the ground and wanders around the yard, you don't have stimulus control. Stimulus control happens once a behavior has been fully trained and is then put on cue. The cue is the 'releasing stimulus' that encourages the behavior to occur.

When we think of using stimulus control with our dogs we often think of verbal phrases or directions ("stay", "come", "sit", etc.) However, dogs are much more tuned into our body language and movement than to verbal language. For this reason, physical signals can also be used to control the performance of behaviors. Hand and arm signals are commonly used. Many dogs are so attentive to our physical motion and movement that even slight changes in head position or shoulder rotation are enough to change their behavior. In the sport of agility, dogs are trained to respond to the handlers' physical positioning and body language in order to move in the desired direction and take the correct obstacle in a sequence.

We can certainly teach our dogs to respond to both verbal cues and body signals. It is important that we teach them in a clear and comprehensive manner, and that we use them in a consistent fashion. Your dog can easily become confused if the cues and signals are not clear and precise. This idea will be discussed further in the following sections.

III. 'Generalization' and 'Discrimination'

In clicker training we talk about cues or signals rather than commands. This distinction is very important. Traditional trainers give

commands. A command must be obeyed at all times or there will be unpleasant consequences. In contrast, a cue or signal means that, if the desired behavior is performed, it will be reinforced. The cue or signal gives the dog an opportunity to perform the behavior and to possibly earn reinforcement. If the behavior has been properly taught, a cue or signal is rarely ignored without good reason.

You can connect any cue or signal with any behavior. Most of us use those that seem the most logical. We use "down" when we want the dog to lie down. However, you could use "drop" or "splat!" or "duck!" if you wanted. A common hand signal for the down is to use a sweeping motion, palm down, towards the floor. However, there is no rule that says that you must use this signal. You could point or wave instead. As long as you connect the cue with the behavior in a systematic fashion (see below) you can use any cue you would like. For most behaviors, it can be helpful to teach both a verbal cue and a hand signal. The verbal cue is most likely to attract the attention of a distracted dog. In noisy situations or at a distance, however, a hand signal may be more useful.

Using Hand Signals

Many people are very impressed by a dog who responds to hand singals. Friends and neighbors are usually astounded when your dog performs without verbal prompting or cues. In reality, it is much easier to teach and use hand signals than to teach and use verbal cues (but you don't need to tell people this!)

To teach many behaviors, you will probably use a food lure. When you use the lure, you are moving it in a specific motion to entice your dog to move into a certain position. The hand movement that accompanies the lure becomes an early signal to your dog. This early hand signal can be used to help prompt the desired behavior even when the food lure is not present. It can then be modified over time to become a distinct hand signal. For example, a sit can be lured by moving a treat up and slightly over the dog's head. The accompanying hand motion will soon elicit the sit even without the lure. Over a number of trials you may then move your hand a bit further away or off to the side, but use the same basic motion to signal the sit. Over time, your sit signal may end up being off to your side and quite some distance from the dog.

Adding Verbal Cues

In clicker training we only add the verbal cue once the behavior is occurring on a regular basis. We want to have the desired behavior first, then we give it a name. This is the opposite of what happens in most traditional types of training. In many training methods, the cue is used from the very beginning, before the dog has any idea what it means. The cue is given and the dog is lured or forced into the behavior over and over again, until the dog eventually makes a connection between the cue and the behavior. There are two major problems with this technique. First, many

The hand movement that accompanies the lure becomes an early signal to your dog…

people assume that their dogs understand the verbal cues long before they actually do. This leads them to have unrealistic expectations about how their dogs should respond. Even if you say "sit" a hundred times as you lure your dog into the sit, that doesn't mean he's made the connection between the word and the behavior. Second, once you name a behavior, that behavior seems to 'freeze' and stay the same from that point on. If you don't have the ultimate version of the behavior that you desire, naming it prematurely can be a problem.

When adding a verbal cue to a lured behavior you want to present it just before the hand motion/signal. Wait a few seconds between the cue and the signal. The slight pause between the verbal cue and the hand signal gives your dog a moment to process the verbal information. As you continue pairing the two, you will find that your dog begins to respond during the slight pause before the hand signal.

When adding a verbal cue or hand signal to a shaped behavior you will start using the cue just as you see the dog beginning to perform the behavior. You don't want to repeat the cue/signal, so, at first, wait until you are fairly certain that the dog is committed to performing the behavior. Over time, you can move the cue/signal earlier and earlier, until it comes before the behavior, rather than as the behavior is starting. For example, let's say that you have been shaping your dog to lift his left front paw to wave. At first you will add the cue/signal once you see that he has begun to lift his paw off the ground. I use the verbal cue "bye-bye" and a side-to-side hand wave as a signal for this behavior. (Each was taught separately). As your dog confidently and correctly 'waves' at you, move the cue/signal earlier so that it precedes the behavior rather than overlaps it.

KEY CONCEPT: In clicker training we add the verbal cue AFTER the dog has learned, and is regularly performing, the desired behavior.

Changing Cues

You may decide to change or add cues for a number of reasons. One reason to change a cue might be that it was added too soon, and the behavior is not what you would like it to be. Many people attempt to teach their dogs to walk on a leash by saying "heel", jerking on the leash, and starting to walk. While some dogs do figure out that they need to get moving when they hear "heel" so they can avoid the jerk on the leash; many others do not. Instead, they learn that "heel" is the signal that an unpleasant event (leash jerk) is about to occur. To try and avoid the leash jerk they try to hang back, away from the handler, when they hear the cue to "heel". When this happens the dog has learned the exact opposite of what the trainer intended. This problem has occurred, in part, because the cue was added before the behavior was learned. The cue to "heel" now means 'hang back to try to avoid the leash jerk'. The easiest way to fix this problem is to stop using the cue altogether. The cue will always hold that original meaning for the dog. Instead, first retrain the behavior in a positive manner (described below). Once the desired walking on leash behavior is attained, give it a new cue ("let's go!", "walkies", etc.)

Another example of this problem is the case in which "Fido, come!" often leads to the dog running as fast as possible in the opposite direction. While we know intellectually that the meaning of "come" is 'move towards me', it is clear from Fido's behavior that "come" means 'run away fast'. Instead of trying to continue using a very flawed cue, it is better to start retraining recalls positively and add a fresh, uncontaminated cue such as "here" or "with me".

Another reason to change a cue might simply be personal preference. You might decide that you no longer want to use an established cue and would like to teach another instead. This is a relatively easy process. Simply follow the pattern of 'new cue, pause for two seconds, old cue'. Your dog will soon learn the sequence and will begin to offer the behavior during the pause. This pattern can be used with either verbal cues, hand signals, or a combination of the two. As your dog begins to respond before the old cue, you can gradually fade it out.

In training tricks, I will often change a cue to something I think is cuter or more appropriate. For example, I taught my Papillon, Copper, to scratch furiously at a spot on my leg when I told him to "dig". I would NOT suggest trying this with a big, strong dog! Then I decided that the cue "I've got an ITCH right here" would be funnier. Long ago I taught my Laborador Retriever, Katie, to weave around and between my legs in a figure eight fashion on the cue 'twist'. I then decided to change the cue to "what does a KITTY-CAT do?" This seemed to make the trick much more entertaining.

I.V. A Basic Training Plan

Most dogs and owners benefit from mastering some basic obedience behaviors. These include watch me (attention), position changes (sit, down, stand), wait/stay, come (recall), and walk on a loose leash. With these behaviors in place, most dogs can be controlled fairly easily. Each of these behaviors needs to be taught in small increments, following six basic steps. Until you have worked through each step, a behavior is not fully taught. For each behavior, the six basic steps are as follows:

1. Get the behavior. You can get the behavior to happen through shaping, luring, or targeting.

2. Reinforce the behavior with a click and a treat/toy/play.

3. If luring or targeting, fade the lure or target.

4. Increase the criteria (duration, distance, distraction).

5. Once the behavior is occurring regularly, add the verbal cue (name it).

6. Move to variable reinforcement. Reinforce every second correct behavior, then every third. Then move to even more random reinforcement.

We will work through each of these six steps for each of the basic behaviors we want to train.

WATCH ME (attention):

One of the most important behaviors you can teach your dog is to look at you and pay attention to you. It's impossible to train a dog who isn't paying attention, so this is an essential foundation behavior to teach.

1. GET THE BEHAVIOR. You can get your dog to watch you in one of two ways: shaping or luring.

To shape attention you should be prepared with your clicker and treats, and simply wait for your dog to look at you. The most difficult thing about this training technique is that the trainer has to wait for the behavior, rather than try to prompt or encourage it.

To lure attention show your dog a treat by putting it on his nose, then move the treat up towards your face. Your dog should look up towards the treat and your face.

2. REINFORCE THE BEHAVIOR. If you are shaping attention click and treat when your dog looks in your general direction. Your ultimate goal is for your dog to look at your face, but start with the dog looking at any part of you.

If you are luring attention click and treat when your dog's eyes follow the treat up towards your face. Your dog will be looking at the treat, not your face, but that's okay at first.

3. FADE THE LURE. Once your dog is regularly looking up when you move the lure towards your face it is time to start fading out the food. To fade the lure, first lure the behavior once and click and treat. Then, make the same hand motion (as if you were holding the lure) with no food in your hand. Your dog is very likely to follow the hand motion with his eyes. When he does, click and take the treat from your pocket or pack for him. Continue fading the lure over several training sessions. Do one or two lured trials, then one or two without the lure. Eventually, only use the lure for every fifth or sixth trial. From there, you can completely fade out its use.

4. INCREASE THE CRITERIA. The three main criteria for any behavior are duration (time), distance, and distraction. It is important to only work on one criteria at any given time. When working on one criteria, make the other two as easy as possible.

To increase duration, simply delay the time between the occurrence of the behavior and the click and treat. At first, wait only a second between the time your dog looks at you and the time you click and treat. Gradually increase the time your dog must continuously perform the behavior before you click. Don't make big leaps in your expectations, proceed slowly. If your dog looks at you, but looks away before you click, do nothing. That trial was unsuccessful and cannot be salvaged. On the next trial, lower your expectations so that your dog can be successful, then slowly raise them again. If you are having repeated failures, stop training. Don't dig yourself into a deeper hole! Maybe your dog is having a bad day, maybe your timing is off, maybe the environment is too distracting, maybe the alignment of planets is causing the problem. There are plenty of reasons for having a bad training session. The best plan of action in these cases is to take a break and try again later.

Whenever you are raising criteria, don't always make it harder for your dog to succeed. Go back and reinforce easier versions of the behavior on a random basis. If your dog is typically able to maintain attention for fifteen seconds, throw in a couple of five second trials during the session. It is hard to maintain enthusiasm and motivation if things always get harder and harder. Planning several trials where your dog has some quick and easy success will help him to maintain a positive attitude about training.

Once you have duration then you will probably want to work on distance. While having your dog pay attention to you when you are right next to him is useful, having him pay attention when you are further away allows for higher level training. Remember, when you start working on distance, drop your duration requirements. To begin training your dog to watch you with distance, take no more than one-half step away from your dog, and immediately click and treat if he continues pay attention to you. Increase your distance from your dog by half-steps. Many dogs will want to follow you when you move away. This exercise is focused on attention, not on training the dog to stay. To avoid problems with a dog who keeps moving, you may want

Reasonable distractions include other people, animals, noises, crowds, etc...

to find some way to restrain the dog (either with a tether, having someone else hold the leash, or leaving the dog behind a barrier as you move away).

Once you have worked on duration and distance, the next criterion is distraction. Consider the types of distractions you would like your dog to ignore in the real world. Reasonable distractions include other people, other animals, noises, crowds, etc. To train your dog to ignore those distractions, start by exposing him to a very mild level of a particular stimulus. Have a person walk by at a distance at first. Your dog will probably notice and look toward the person, then look back at you. Reinforce immediately for looking back at you. When your dog is able to ignore the distraction at that level, have the person move closer and closer (as long as your dog is able to be successful). When your dog is able to ignore a person approaching him and continue paying attention to you, move to a different distraction. Next, you might have a person with a dog walk by at a distance. As your dog is able to ignore them and watch you, they can move closer and closer.

You will probably have to go out into different environments to complete your distraction training. Parking lots and public parks are good places to train. Start out by practicing attention at a distance from the action and gradually move closer and closer as your dog seems ready. If you have several unsuccessful trials you can move further away and try again.

Next, you will want to begin combining criteria. I typically start with duration and distance. Let's say my goal is to have my dog watch me for thirty seconds while I am fifteen steps away. The time it takes to reach this goal varies depending on the dog and trainer. It may take several sessions over several days, or it may take a week of training every other day. It's important not to get caught up in goals such as 'we MUST be at this level by such and such a date or time'. Putting time pressure on yourself and your dog can lead to stress and frustration. Learning occurs at its own pace.

I have already taught each of these criteria (duration and distance) separately, and now I am ready to put them together. To begin, I will choose a moderately easy level for one criteria while I work on increasing the other. Let's say that I decide to work at a distance of five steps while I increase duration requirements. I'll probably start out at five steps with a duration of three seconds. If that

is easy for my dog, I'll move up to a duration of five seconds. I'm clicking and treating each successful trial, then starting again. I will continue building duration while at five steps, occasionally throwing in an easy trial or two. When I have reached my duration goal of thirty seconds at five steps I will then increase distance and decrease duration. Now I will go to seven steps at three seconds and continue working at that distance level to increase duration back up to thirty seconds. Next I may move to ten steps at three seconds. I would continue building the duration and distance criteria in this manner. If the behavior 'breaks down' at any level, and my dog is unable to be successful, I would simply drop back to an easier version of the behavior and begin building again.

Once I have reached my goal of thirty seconds of attention while I am fifteen steps away, I would add in distractions while decreasing duration and distance to a moderate level. At this point I may feel that my dog is easily paying attention to me for fifteen seconds while I am eight steps away (this is about half of what my dog has been doing without distractions). Now I will add very mild distractions while my other two criteria remain at a moderate level. If my dog is successful I will continue to work up to more and more difficult distractions while keeping duration and distance constant. Then I would increase distance and duration slightly (eighteen seconds at ten steps), and drop back down to mild distractions, working my way up to more difficult ones again. If your dog is having trouble being successful, it may be necessary to decrease the other criteria (separately) to an easier level. You might decide to drop duration requirements by half for a few trials then increase it again.

When increasing criteria the basic pattern is to first train each criterion separately to the desired level. Then combine two of the criteria, starting with one being held constant at a moderate level while the other starts out very low and is systematically increased. Then you slightly increase the criterion that was being held constant and start from the beginning with the other, systematically increasing it to desired levels again. Finally, you hold two criteria constant at a moderate level while introducing and increasing the third. This sounds much more complicated than it actually is! When you are training, you will get a feel for when your dog is ready to move on and when he needs more practice at a particular level. Don't ever be hesitant to decrease criteria to an easier level if your dog is having trouble being successful. Simply drop back for a few trials, then start increasing your expectations again.

5. ADD A VERBAL CUE. Most people use a verbal cue such as "watch me" or "look" for attention. Add this cue at the beginning of the behavior once your dog is regularly offering attention. At first, use the cue as your dog begins looking at you. After your dog has heard the cue associated with the behavior a number of times, you can start to use it before the behavior is offered. Don't repeat the cue! It is not a mantra "watch me, watch me, watch me, watch me, watch me, watch me, watch

me, watch me..." It should only be given once for any trial.

6. MOVE TO VARIABLE REINFORCEMENT. Once you have completed all the previous steps you can move to variable reinforcement. Ask your dog to watch you for a few seconds, then praise and release "good watch, OK". You might have to move to get your dog to look away. Then, set your dog up again at the same level. This time click and treat for a successful trial. You have just gotten a 2-fer (this term comes from Karen Pryor). A 2-fer is two behaviors for the price of one. Next you might ask for two behaviors with just a praise and release, then click and treat the third one (a 3-fer!)

In order for reinforcement to become truly variable, it needs to be random and unpredictable. You might reinforce two or three behaviors in a row with a click and treat, then simply praise and release the next two. Then you might click and treat one behavior, then ask for three more that are praised and released. You will continue expecting more and more behaviors for less and less reinforcement, occasionally throwing in a few reinforced trials in a row.

POSITION CHANGES (sit, down, stand):

The three body positions (sit, down, stand) have many common elements. Each is a passive, static behavior. Each is trained in a similar fashion. Our ultimate goal is the same; to have the dog move into the desired position and then hold that position until told otherwise. In teaching each of these positions we will follow the same basic steps.

SIT:

1. GET THE BEHAVIOR. The easiest way to get a sit to happen is to lure it with food. Most dogs very happily follow a smelly treat with their noses. If you move the treat up and back slightly (sort of over and between your dog's eyes), his nose will follow and move upward, and his rear end will move down into a sit. A little practice with correct hand position might be required at first.

2. REINFORCE THE BEHAVIOR. When your dog moves into the sit position, click (keeping the clicker away from your dog's ears) and give him the lure.

3. FADE THE LURE. Once your dog will regularly follow the food lure and move into a sitting position you will need to fade the lure. To do this lure and reinforce the sit several times. Then use the same hand motion you've been using to lure, but without the food in your hand. Most dogs will follow the hand motion. When your dog sits, click and take a treat from your pocket or pack for him.

4. INCREASE THE CRITERIA. Now it's time to increase the criteria until you reach the desired final behavior. It is very important to only increase one criterion (duration, distance, distraction) at a time. For a steady sit you will probably want to increase duration first. Once your dog is sitting, wait for several seconds before you click and treat. Slowly lengthen the time that you wait (by seconds) before you click and treat.

Remember, the click not only means that your dog performed the correct behavior and that a reinforcer is now available, it also means that your dog is released from the position. This means he's allowed to move after he hears the click. This is fine because it allows you the opportunity to reset for the next trial.

Once you have the duration you want, you can then work on increasing your distance from your dog while he sits. When you raise this criterion, lower your duration requirement. You may need to move away from your dog very slowly in order for him to maintain the sit. If your dog gets up, you need to move away in smaller increments. For some dogs, you may need to simply turn your head or bend forward. If your dog remains steady, click and treat. At first move no more than one-half step away, immediately move back, click and treat. Do this several times. Then move one step away, immediately move back, click and treat. Increase distance after several successful trials. Every 5-6 trials, reinforce an easier version of the behavior (shorter distance). Continue working in this manner until your dog will remain sitting as you take 6-8 steps away and immediately return.

Next, introduce distraction. Remember, you must now decrease the other criteria (duration and distance). Stay right next to your dog while someone walks by at a reasonable distance. You don't want the distraction too close at first. Click and treat BEFORE your dog has a chance to get up and investigate. Add distractions in small doses, always striving to keep the distraction small enough to allow your dog to be successful. Distractions can be people, animals, food, toys, and different environments.

Finally, once you have separately trained your dog to the levels of duration, distance, and distraction that you desire, you can combine two of the elements at a time. Make each criteria as easy as possible when first combining them. For example, you might combine distance and distraction by moving two steps away from your dog while a mild distraction appears at a distance. You would then immediately move back and reinforce. For the next trial you might move further away while the same mild distraction appears. Or, you might stay at the same distance, and make the distraction more appealing. You might then combine duration and distance by increasing first one, then the other. For example, you might take five steps away from your dog, wait three seconds, return and reinforce. Then you might take seven steps away, wait three seconds, return and reinforce. Work in this manner until you are at your desired distance. Then go back to five steps, wait five seconds, return and reinforce. Continue to move slightly further away after each successful five second sit. Then you can move on to seven second sits at each of the distances, etc.

By working in this fashion, you can make relatively steady progress. However, if your dog begins to have trouble at any level, go

Strive to keep the distractions small enough to allow your dog to be successful...

back to an easier version of the behavior for a few trials, then slowly raise your criteria again. The goal is to help the dog be successful at every step and to avoid failures as much as possible. A failure means that the dog was unable to meet the requirements for that trial. As a good trainer, you need to keep your expectations reasonable and set criteria that are attainable for your dog at any given time. You need to have a general idea of which criteria you are working on within any training session, and what your short and long-term goals are for each exercise. For example, you may have reached the point where your dog will hold a twenty second sit while you are five steps away. Your goal for that session might be to increase your distance to ten steps while maintaining the twenty second sit. Your goal for that week might be to increase the duration of the sit to thirty seconds while you are fifteen steps away. Your long-term goal might be to teach a one minute sit while you are thirty steps away.

5. ADD A VERBAL CUE. The verbal cue to "sit" should be added immediately before the hand motion/signal that you have been using. Give the verbal cue, wait one or two seconds, then give the hand signal.

6. MOVE TO VARIABLE REINFORCEMENT. Once you have worked through the previous steps, it is time to move to variable, rather than continuous, reinforcement. Start by asking for the sit once, then praise and release the dog — "good sit, OK". You might have to move slightly to get your dog to leave the sit position. Then cue the sit again, and click and treat. You've just gotten two sits for one click and treat.

The key to successfully moving to variable reinforcement is that the reinforcement becomes random and unexpected. If you continue to always reinforce every second sit, your reinforcement is predictable and systematic. Instead, sometimes reinforce two sits in a row and other times ask for three sits before reinforcement. As your dog is able to continue performing successfully, continue randomizing reinforcement while asking for more unreinforced repetitions. For example: sit, click & treat; sit, release; sit, release; sit, click & treat; sit, release; sit, release; sit, release; sit, click & treat; sit, click & treat;.....

DOWN:

1. GET THE BEHAVIOR. As with the sit, the down position is usually fairly easy to lure using a food treat. One important thing to

be aware of is that the down seems like a completely different behavior to the dog depending on his starting position (sit or stand). Moving to the down from the sit requires the dog to move his body forward as he lies down. Moving to the down from the stand requires the dog to fold his body backwards as he lies down. For many people this distinction is not important. However, if you ever intend to participate in competition obedience or agility, you will want to be sure to teach the down from both positions. In these activities, there is an advantage to having the dog down from the stand.

To teach down from the sit, put the food lure directly in front of your dog's nose and move it straight down to the floor (between his front feet), then slowly move it slightly forward along the floor (the hand motion with the lure resembles an L shape).

To teach down from the stand, put the food lure directly in front of your dog's nose and move it under his chin and towards his chest (a pushing towards the dog motion). The dog should fold backwards into the down position. This is sometimes called an accordion down.

If you are teaching both of these variations you will want to teach them separately. Don't practice them together in your training sessions. You will also want to give them different verbal cues.

Sometimes it will be very difficult to lure a dog into a down. I've often seen this happen with very small dogs. They are close to the floor already and don't seem to see the point of lying down! For these dogs you might work on simply capturing the down when it naturally occurs and reinforcing it. This means you must be ready to click and treat at all times.

You might try luring the dog under something like a low table. You can also sit on the floor with your legs straight out in front of you and bend one leg slightly at the knee, leaving enough space for your dog to crawl under, and try luring your dog under your leg.

2. REINFORCE THE BEHAVIOR. As soon as your dog moves into the down position, click and treat (give him the lure). At first, your dog may offer a partial down (bending into a bow with elbows down). Reinforce the partial downs a few times to let him know he's heading in the right direction, then wait for the rear end to go down as well.

3. FADE THE LURE. Follow the same directions as in fading the lure for the sit. The hand motion now becomes a signal to perform the behavior, even when the lure is not present. Randomly practice a series of lured and empty hand (no lure present) trials. Gradually reduce the number of lured trials. Continue to click and treat every successful trial.

4. INCREASE THE CRITERIA. You will increase your criteria for the down just as you did for the sit. First work on duration, then distance, then distraction. Then combine two of the criteria, and finally, combine all three. Remember to work in a systematic fashion and to always make it possible for your dog to be successful at any given level before raising your requirements.

As my business partner, Liz, often says "people want to teach the dog to lay down and stay for 30 minutes while they leave the room and have a marching band come through". What she means is that people often raise all the requirements to exceedingly high levels, and combine them, way too soon. Doing this leads to repeated failures which are unpleasant and disappointing for both the trainer and the dog. It is certainly possible to teach the dog to remain in a position even when the handler is gone and there are high levels of distraction, but you have to build that behavior slowly and carefully.

5. ADD A VERBAL CUE. Once your dog is moving into the down position whenever you use the hand motion, add the verbal cue to "down" just before you use the hand motion/signal. The verbal cue should precede the hand motion by several seconds. Give the verbal cue, wait for a few seconds, then give the hand signal.

6. MOVE TO VARIABLE REINFORCEMENT. Follow the same directions as described in teaching the sit (above). Start out asking for two behaviors for one click and treat. Then you can ask for three. Then start randomizing by clicking and treating two behaviors in a row, then asking for three or four unreinforced behaviors.

If your dog ever seems confused or stops offering

the behavior when given the cue, you should drop back to a level of higher reinforcement for a few trials, then slowly start randomizing again. You might do three behaviors, all reinforced, then two that are not, then two that are. If that goes well, try asking for three unreinforced behaviors, one reinforced, etc. As with raising criteria, you will get a feel for when your dog needs more reinforcement and when you can ask him for more unreinforced trials.

STAND:

1. GET THE BEHAVIOR. You can get your dog to stand either by luring or targeting. To lure the stand put the lure on his nose and move it straight out in front of the dog. Your hand position is very important here. If it's too high your dog will sit; too low and he will lie down.

If you have already taught your dog to target your hand, you can ask him to touch your palm when it is held so that your dog must stand in order to do so.

2. REINFORCE THE BEHAVIOR. As soon as your dog is standing still (even for a second!) on all four feet, click and treat.

3. FADE THE LURE. If you are using a food lure to elicit this behavior, fade it out systematically. If you have used a hand target for this behavior, you can skip this step.

4. INCREASE THE CRITERIA. Increase the criteria for the stand as you did for the sit and the down. First increase duration requirements, then distance, then distractions. You may find that it is more difficult for your dog to hold a steady stand than either a sit or a down. It is much easier to start moving from the stand position than from the other two body positions. You may have to increase your criteria more slowly for the stand.

5. ADD A VERBAL CUE. Add the verbal cue "stand" just before you give the hand motion/signal for your dog to move to the stand position. Remember, don't add the cue too soon. Your dog should be consistently and quickly moving into the stand on the hand signal before you start adding the cue. The sequence should be verbal cue, slight pause, hand signal.

6. MOVE TO VARIABLE REINFORCEMENT. Follow the same directions described in teaching the sit and down. An important point to remember is that reinforcement is information. The click and treat communicate to your dog that he has correctly performed the desired behavior. When we phase out continuous reinforcement, we are also removing continuous feedback. If your dog seems unsure, he may still need the information that continuous reinforcement provides. Don't think of it as moving backwards, think of it as laying a stronger foundation.

WAIT/STAY:

Many people don't make any distinction between a wait and a stay. However, I teach these two exercises as completely different behaviors. The wait is used when I want my dog to hold still for a very short duration. When the wait is over my dog can move out of position and resume activity. The stay is usually of a longer duration. My dog may not move from the stay position until I return and formally release him. If I'm walking in the front door I might ask my dog to "wait" while I fumble with my keys, open the door, and walk through. This cue means that I expect him to hold his position for a few seconds. Then I would tell him "OK" to allow him to follow me in. If I am working with a student in a training class I might ask my dog to "down" and to "stay". This means that I expect him to be in that position for a little while, and that I will return to him before he is allowed to move.

Early training for these two behaviors is similar, but it is clearer to the dog if you keep them as different and separate as possible. Teach them in different training sessions. Better yet, teach one first, then the other. For both of these behaviors, it is important that you work at the level at which your dog can be successful. If your dog is continually unable to gain reinforcement, you need to make your requirements for success as easy as possible. For some dogs, holding still and doing nothing is the most difficult thing we can ask of them!

If you have already taught the position changes, you have already taught your dog to wait and stay for short time increments. Now you will simply need to name and refine those behaviors.

The wait is used when I want my dog to hold still for a short duration...

1. GET THE BEHAVIOR. The wait/stay is simply a matter of duration in any one of the three body positions. Once the positions are on cue you can ask for one of them.

2. REINFORCE THE BEHAVIOR. As always, click and treat once the desired behavior has been performed.

3. FADE THE LURE. By the time you get to wait/stay training, you should not be using a lure. Trying to use a food lure for these exercises will be counterproductive. Your dog will try to follow the lure and will not hold still.

4. INCREASE THE CRITERIA. Think about

the situations in which you are likely to use wait or stay, and design your training sessions based on those goals. For the wait you want short duration, short distance, and moderate to high distraction. For the stay you want longer duration, longer distance, and high distraction. My ultimate version of a 'wait' is for my dog to hold whatever position he was left in for less than a minute while I move a short distance away. However, there may be a number of possible distractions in that time that he needs to ignore. My ultimate version of a 'stay' is for my dog to hold whatever position he was left in no matter what happens. I may go out of sight and there may be distractions while I am gone. When I return I expect my dog to be in the same position he was left in.

With these exercises it is very important to randomly reinforce your dog for easier versions of the behavior from time to time. The wait and stay require quite a bit of self-control and concentration from your dog. Give them some easy successes instead of always making it harder.

I have seen many people attempt to increase duration on a wait/stay by clicking and treating, but expecting the dog to remain in position and continue the exercise. This is sending mixed signals to the dog, as the click also means the dog is released from that training trial. Increase duration with multiple trials of slowly increasing time demands. It is more useful to practice ten short trials ranging from five to twenty seconds each than to try to do one long trial of thirty seconds with failure.

5. ADD A VERBAL CUE. I use the cues "wait" and "stay" for these behaviors. I have heard all kinds of possibilities include "chill out", "settle" and "plant it". Be sure that your verbal cues for the two behaviors are distinctly different. Don't add the verbal cue until you are 99% sure that your dog is going to hold the position until released. This is another case in which people want to repeat the cue over and over and over ("stay, stay, stay, stay, stay, stay, stay...") Don't do this! If you fall into this habit, you will only confuse your dog. If he's already staying, he doesn't need to be told again and again while he's doing it. If he isn't staying, you need to decrease your criteria in order to be successful. You may also need to stop using the verbal cue until the behavior is solid.

6. MOVE TO VARIABLE REINFORCEMENT. When your dog will consistently hold a wait/stay in a calm and steady manner, you can move to variable reinforcement. For 'wait' I may simply release the dog when I am at a distance with a "good wait, OK!" For 'stay' I always return to the dog to release him. I also touch my dogs lightly on the head during the release from a stay. This is a clear signal that the stay is over and they can now move.

COME (recall):

One of the most important things you can teach your dog is to come to you when he is called. Start recall training as early as possible and never take it for granted. You will spend your dog's entire life maintaining this behavior.

A good recall could mean the difference between life and death for your dog, so take it very seriously. If you make coming to you fun, exciting, and rewarding, you can train a very solid and reliable recall.

1. GET THE BEHAVIOR. The easiest way to get your dog to come to you is to make it worthwhile for him to do so. At first, you can lure him to you with treats or toys. Start with your dog at a very short distance from you in a setting with no distractions. Show him your lure and encourage him to come and get it. When he comes, click and give him his treat or play with him with his toy.

In Your Face Recalls

A fun and easy way to start making the recall a positive experience for your dog is to practice 'in your face' recalls. This is one case when I make an exception to adding the verbal cue early. I make this exception because the exercise makes it impossible for the dog to get it wrong and not respond to the cue in the early stages of training. Also, this exercise involves conditioning (training) a very positive response to the verbal cue used for a recall.

To practice 'in your face' recalls get your clicker and the best possible treats you can find. Have a large quantity of small, soft, smelly treats readily available. In a setting with no distractions stand right in front of your dog, being sure you have his attention. Say his name, then your recall cue, click, and pop a treat in his mouth. At this point you are not asking your dog to do anything except take and swallow the treat. But you are teaching him that hearing his name followed by your recall cue is a very good thing because it leads to reinforcement. Continue this exercise in every room in your house, then take it outside to practice. At first, always practice with no/low distractions, being sure you are right in front of your dog. He should not have to move towards you at all yet. Once your dog responds positively whenever your practice this exercise in different settings, then you can slowly add distance. Start by being only one step away, so your dog simply has to move slightly towards you to gain reinforcement. Increase distance as your dog remains successful.

Treat Recalls

Another fun game to play that teaches your dog a good recall is the 'treat recall'. For this game it helps to have treats that are round (Planter's Cheese Balls™ and Kix Cereal™ are two examples). These roll well and your dog will enjoy chasing them. Show your dog a treat, throw it a short distance, and encourage him to chase it and eat it. When he finishes that treat show him another and encourage him to come back to you to get it. Click and treat when he comes to you. Repeat this exercise, throwing treats away from you in various directions and at varying distances. You might have better treats for coming to you than for running away to chase them. This will teach your dog that coming to you is a very beneficial behavior.

Automatic Recalls

You will probably have many opportunities to reinforce your dog for coming to you, even when you did not ask him to. Don't let these opportunities pass by! Whenever your dog 'checks in' by looking to you or moving towards you, reinforce that behavior. If you don't have a clicker and treats, use lots of praise, petting, and play. You want checking in with you and coming to you to become a habit.

You can practice automatic recalls in your house and yard. Simply be ready to reinforce anytime your dog offers you attention or moves towards you. I use this exercise when I take my dogs out to run in a large enclosed field (don't do this until you have a reliable recall already). When I first let them loose to run I give them each a really good treat. Then, whenever they return to me voluntarily they get several more treats. By the end of our outings, they are typically spending more time with me than they are out exploring. The dog learns to assume responsibility for keeping an eye on and staying close to the owner.

2. REINFORCE THE BEHAVIOR. Always, always, always, make responding to a recall a pleasant event. If you are going to do anything unpleasant to your dog (put him in his crate, cut his nails, etc.), don't call him to you, go get him instead. Keep your dog's attitude about coming to you enthusiastic by having different and desirable reinforcers for successful recalls.

3. FADE THE LURE. If your dog only comes to you when he sees a treat or toy, you do not have a reliable recall. Fade out the obvious lure by alternating lured recalls with non-lured ones. Show your dog a treat, call him, click and give him the treat. Then call him without showing the treat, and click and treat when he comes to you. Vary your lured and non-lured recalls randomly. Sometimes you can show him the lure, but not give it to him when he comes. Instead, praise him and play with him. On the next trial, don't show him the lure, but click and treat when he responds. Many dogs have learned that the lure means they will get reinforced and no lure means they will not. Don't fall into this pattern. Instead, sometimes a lure means no food, sometimes no lure means food. Keep your dog guessing.

4. INCREASE THE CRITERIA. The important criteria for a recall are distance and distraction. Work on distance first, in low distraction situations. You might call your dog from across the room, then from around the corner in the hallway, then from different rooms, then from upstairs or downstairs. ALWAYS reinforce highly. Two family members can call the dog back and forth between them from different rooms, each having a great reinforcer.

When you add distraction to the recall do it slowly and carefully. Make sure to decrease distance when you begin distraction training. Consider the things that might be low, moderate, and high level distractions for your dog. A low level distraction might be another person in the room, but ignoring the dog. A moderate level distraction might be several children playing next door. A high level distraction might be another dog in the area. Each dog will be different in terms of what is most distracting. For example, my Golden Retriever finds any person to be a very high distraction as he's sure they want to meet and greet him. My Laborador Retriever, however, can easily ignore people, but not squirrels.

In distraction training for the recall, it's a good idea to have your dog on a leash at first. The leash will limit your dog's ability to make a mistake. As you continue recall training you might want to use a long line or a retractable leash (such as a Flexi lead) so that you can get more distance while keeping your dog safe and limiting his choices.

If your dog ignores a recall cue the leash allows you to move towards him or to bring him towards you quickly and easily. On the next trial you may need to make your distractions lower by changing the environment in some way. You may need to move further away from the distraction. For example, imagine that you have your dog on a long line and you are practicing recalls at the park where a kid's soccer game is going on. You would start out working at a distance from the action, gradually moving closer and closer as your dog responds successfully. If you get to the place where your dog is unable to ignore the running, screaming children, you may need to move further away, or behind a barrier such as a row of trees or bleachers.

It is important to avoid recall failures in your

In distraction training for the recall, it's a good idea to have your dog on a leash at first...

training. They will happen from time to time, but every instance in which your dog does not come when called is a moment of 'untraining'.

5. ADD A VERBAL CUE. As I said earlier, the recall is one exception that I make to the rule that you wait until the behavior is being regularly performed before you add the cue. Because of this, it is extremely important to be very careful in how you use the cue. Only use the verbal cue when you are 99% sure that your dog is going to come when you use it. If you find yourself running after your dog yelling "Fido, come!" as he happily heads in the opposite direction, you are 'untraining' the verbal cue. At the moment, do whatever it takes to get your dog back (and don't punish him once you catch him!) In the future, use better management to avoid such situations. In addition, use positive methods to strengthen

the recall. Also, avoid repeating the verbal cue. It's a one-time offer. Don't offer reinforcement if the first verbal cue to come was ignored. If your dog does not respond appropriately the first time you need to work on recalls with lower distractions and better reinforcers.

Everyone who interacts with the dog should use the same verbal cue. Family members can practice a 'recall game' in which each person is armed with a clicker and treats. People take turns calling the dog, then clicking and treating when he responds. This can be a 'round robin' type activity in which the dog is randomly called from one person to another very quickly. Practicing this game helps teach the dog to respond to verbal cues from all members of the household.

6. MOVE TO VARIABLE REINFORCEMENT. Move to variable reinforcement for recalls very, very slowly. To begin, you might call your dog to you, then praise and release. Next, call your dog to you, click and treat. Then call your dog to you, praise and play. Then call your dog to you, click and treat. Then do 2 recalls where you praise and release followed by one where you click and treat. Keep your dog guessing about what good thing might happen when he responds to a recall cue.

LOOSE LEASH WALKING:

Everyone wants a dog who walks nicely on a leash. This can be relatively easy to teach a young dog or puppy, and very difficult to teach an older dog who has already learned to pull. Most dogs who pull have learned that pulling gets them where they want to go. It quickly becomes a self-reinforcing behavior. The harder they pull the faster they get to go somewhere. Once this pattern has been established, breaking it takes determination and patience. Our goal is to teach the dog that pulling means we do not move forward. In fact, we might even move backwards instead. We want a dog who feels his collar tighten to back up and loosen it on his own. Most people assume that the dog will eventually back off and stop pulling if he keeps getting choked by his collar. However, most dogs don't seem to make this connection. Instead, they might even pull harder to try to get away from the pressure. It takes conscious awareness and effort to break this unwanted habit in your dog.

1. GET THE BEHAVIOR.

Loose Leash Standing

The first step to getting loose leash walking is getting your dog to stand still next to you on a loose leash. Surprisingly, this may be harder than it sounds. For many dogs, simply putting on the leash and collar is a signal to start pulling. So step one in getting the behavior is to click and treat your dog for standing within a 4 foot radius of you with a loose leash. It's important that you don't allow the dog to strain at the end of the leash. If he does this, move off slightly to one side or the other. Whenever your dog releases pressure on the leash or moves towards you, click and treat. Remember, the target behavior is 'loose leash', so your dog does not need to be right next to you, or even look at you, in order to earn reinforcement. He simply needs to stand within the 4 foot radius without pulling. Don't start moving with your dog on the leash until you reliably get a loose leash while standing still. When you do start moving, reinforce your dog for every step when the leash is loose.

Luring

You can use a food lure to move your dog close to you while you walk. Choose a preferred side (everyone who walks the dog should use the same side) and use a lure to lead your dog there. Reinforce your dog heavily for being on the preferred side and close to you. Keep the food lure in the hand on the same side as the dog (left hand/left side or right hand/right side) and make sure it is at the dog's nose height. Lead your dog forward a step or two with the lure, then click and treat. Practice often, luring your dog only a few steps at a time.

Penalty Yards

I first learned about the basic concept of this exercise from a trainer named Lana Mitchell. Her description reminded me of the penalty that might be incurred in a football game (hence the name). It also reminded me of the grade school rule in which a child running in the hall is required to go back to the beginning and walk nicely.

In penalty yards, the dog incurs a penalty for having a tight leash, and must go back to the beginning and start over. Begin this exercise by showing the dog a temptation (a person with a toy or treat). Make sure the dog is motivated to reach the temptation (it needs to be something he wants). Have the person playing the temptation stand about 20 feet in front of the dog after showing him the treat or toy. The trainer then starts walking towards the temptation with the dog on leash. When the dog pulls (and most will) to reach the temptation, the trainer starts backing up (saying nothing at all to the dog) all the way to the beginning. If the dog is very strong or determined, the trainer may have to move slightly to one side or the other as she starts moving backwards to throw the dog slightly off balance. Don't jerk the leash, just keep a steady pressure. The trainer should move backwards, NOT turn around and walk the other direction. We want it to be clear to the dog that pulling causes him to move AWAY from the thing that he wants.

Once the trainer and dog move back to the starting place, and the leash is loose, they can begin forward motion again. The handler can praise the dog and click and treat whenever the leash is loose. The handler says nothing when the leash tightens, but immediately moves into reverse and goes clear back to the beginning to try again. We are trying to help the dog make the connection that a tight leash = moving away from your goal. Some dogs pick up on this connection very quickly; others take longer. When using this technique, the trainer needs to be very patient yet very determined. You simply have to keep 'throwing it in reverse' until the dog starts to understand what's happening.

2. REINFORCE THE BEHAVIOR. When teaching loose leash standing and walking, it is vitally important to reinforce each small increment of desirable behavior. Don't try to walk to the end of the block on a loose leash before you reinforce! At first reinforce for simply standing next to you on a loose leash. Then reinforce each attempt the dog makes to stay within the 4 foot radius. Don't expect too much too soon. Also, remember that your reinforcer must be better than the reinforcement your dog gets from pulling.

3. FADE THE LURE. One way to transition your dog away from an obvious lure is to teach your dog to target your luring hand. See Chapter 4 for details on how to teach targeting. You can then practice having your dog walk next to you as he follows the target hand.

4. INCREASE THE CRITERIA. The important criteria for loose leash walking are duration and distraction. You are going to want to increase the time that your dog will continuously perform the behavior (duration). You will then need to increase environmental distraction while the behavior is being performed.

Loose leash walking is one of those situations where It's best to 'make haste slowly'. Getting two or three good steps at a time is better than pushing for five or six steps, and failing. Build

on your dog's success. When you add distraction do so carefully and be sure to decrease duration. For example, you might go to the end of your driveway while the neighbor across the street is out doing yard work. Work on getting two or three steps of loose leash walking. Once your dog is successful at this level several times, go for four or five steps. At your next training session you might increase distraction slightly. For example, you might work in front of your neighbor's house as several children play. Decrease your duration expectations back to two or three steps for the first couple of trials, increasing as your dog does well. Save the really big distractions (squirrels, garbage on the ground, other dogs) until your dog is doing well at the mild, then moderate, levels.

5. ADD THE VERBAL CUE. You can use any number of possible verbal cues for this behavior. Common ones include "heel", "with me", "let's go", and "walkies". At first, add the verbal cue as your dog is performing the behavior, then reinforce. Move the verbal cue earlier and earlier, until it is coming just before the behavior. As always, don't continually repeat the verbal cue. If you do this, it will eventually become meaningless.

6. MOVE TO VARIABLE REINFORCEMENT. Once your dog is performing well with the verbal cue, you can make your reinforcement for loose leash walking more variable and random. Sometimes reinforce after one or two steps. Other times go eight or ten steps for one trial, then three steps for the next, then fifteen

steps, etc. Remember, don't always make it harder for your dog to gain reinforcement. Click and treat when he is not expecting it to keep his enthusiasm and interest high.

A note on the training steps: You can use the basic training plan presented to teach your dog any behavior he is physically and mentally capable of performing. Based on the above examples, it should be relatively easy to break the behavior down into the required steps. Every dog learns every behavior in a slightly different way and at a slightly different rate, but the training steps should provide a good guideline to follow.

Generalization

Generalization is really step seven in your basic training plan for any behavior. To generalize means to respond in spite of a number of different changes in the environment. Some changes are relatively minor and might even go unnoticed by the trainer. There might be an unusual or very enticing smell on the ground. The wind might be blowing in a way that carries an interesting scent. Your dog might be jumpy and nervous because he feels a storm approaching. Something as simple as moving to a different place in the same room, or just facing in a different direction, can have a big impact on your dog's responses. Our goal in generalization training is to practice with enough environmental changes so that our dogs learn to ignore them and continue to respond appropriately to our cues and signals.

Sink or Swim

Many trainers take the sink or swim approach to training. They train a behavior in a relatively low distraction environment (imagine learning to swim in a kiddie pool) and the dog performs well. When they take the dog into a new setting (then imagine being thrown in the ocean) they are surprised when the dog does not perform well, or even at all. This is when the disappointed trainer says 'But he KNOWS how to sit, stay, come, heel, etc.!" Avoid making this mistake. A dog performs what he is capable of performing in any given setting. If he isn't doing it, he doesn't really know it or isn't capable of doing it in that particular situation. One of the main reasons for lack of performance in new settings is a lack of generalization training.

KEY CONCEPT: Poor performance or lack of performance in a new setting is often a lack of generalization.

Proof positive

Traditional trainers often refer to a concept called proofing. Proofing is meant to teach the dog to perform the required behavior despite distractions and environmental changes. While the idea is a good one, the application has sometimes gone terribly wrong. Some trainers approach proofing as a process of tricking the dog into making mistakes so that those mistakes can be corrected. The correction is usually an unpleasant consequence for the dog (punishment). To me, this seems like a very unfair and ineffective approach. When you cause the dog to make an error, then punish it, you are breaking down your dog's trust in you and his enjoyment in the training process.

However, if you approach proofing in a positive manner, it can simply be another step in the process of training reliable behaviors. In reality, proofing is simply adding various distraction criteria to the behavior. If you're following the basic training steps, you have already built-in this phase of training. For certain behaviors, though, you may need to add specialized criteria. For example, if you are training your dog for competition obedience, you need to proof for possibilities such as another dog jumping and retrieving behind your dog while he is on a sit/stay. To build up your dog's ability to ignore such activity, reinforce him heavily while slowly and systematically increasing the level of distractions. You might start by having your dog sit/stay while someone simply walks a dog back and forth about 20 feet behind him. Then you might have someone jog back and forth with a dog at the same distance. Move the distraction closer, decreasing the level of activity first, then increasing it. If your dog makes an error during proofing, you need to go back to an easier level of distraction and move up again.

In positive proofing the dog is not corrected for making mistakes. Instead, he is reinforced for getting it right. This type of positive proofing leads to a dog who happily and confidently performs correctly despite distractions.

Discrimination

Discrimination is the ability to tell the difference between similar stimuli. If you've ever had the experience of having the phone ring in the middle of the night and you've tried to stop the sound by turning off the alarm clock, you've made a discrimination error. Discrimination errors result from confusion between stimuli or signals.

If you use verbal cues that have similar sounds, your dog may find it hard to correctly discriminate between them. In agility training, for example, the cues "tire", "tunnel", and "table" are easily confused. Often the dog only catches the "t" sound and heads for the first obstacle that he sees that starts with that sound, missing the rest of the cue. When using hand signals, your dog may mistake the down signal for the recall signal or the sit signal. The more similar your signals (same hand, same motion, same height, etc.) the more likely your dog will make an error. It is your job as a trainer and handler to make your signals as clear and distinctly different from one another as possible.

KEY CONCEPTS REVISITED:

It is better to find a trainer who truly endorses the concepts of clicker training and positive reinforcement than to take a traditional, force-based training class. A trainer who truly understands and uses positive techniques will work hard to stay true to that focus, even when dealing with behavior problems. A trainer with a more traditional focus will be likely to consider more force-based techniques when faced with problems in training.

In clicker training we add the verbal cue AFTER the dog has learned, and is regularly performing, the desired behavior. The verbal cue serves to 'freeze' the behavior in its current form. Don't add it until the behavior is being performed regularly exactly as you want.

Poor performance or lack of performance in a new setting is often a lack of generalization. A behavior is not really well-learned until it has been generalized in a number of new locations. It is the trainer's responsibility to complete generalization training before expecting the behavior to be performed in a variety of settings.

Every instance in which your dog does not come when called is a moment of 'untraining' ...

For further reading:
The Clicker Workbook: A Beginner's Guide *by Deborah Jones, Ph.D.*
Learning & Behavior *by Paul Chance, Ph.D.*

"The good news is that, using clicker training, it is possible to train your dog to be a good canine citizen in a fun and enjoyable way."

Chapter 7

Rude Dogs

— *Learning to Say "Please"* —

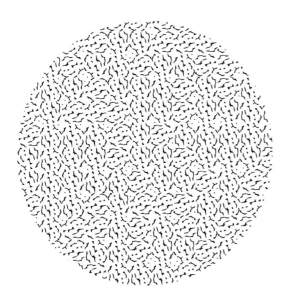

Even though dogs are domesticated, they are not necessarily civilized. Domesticated means that animals of a certain species have been selectively bred over time for those who will be most compatible with human beings. Domesticated animals have the potential to work well and live comfortably with humans. However, having the potential to be a good companion is not an automatic guarantee of a good pet. In addition to being domesticated, a good pet must also be civilized. A civilized dog is one who understands proper and appropriate behavior around humans and other animals.

It is up to us as pet owners to teach our dogs how to live within our expectations and requirements. Many behaviors that are perfectly natural for dogs are labeled as 'bad' by humans. Some of those normal doggie behaviors are even dangerous — jumping on people, running loose, eating non-food items, etc. In order to civilize our pets and to live with them happily we need to find ways to increase the behaviors we desire and to decrease the behaviors we dislike or find unacceptable.

KEY CONCEPT: *It is up to us as pet owners to teach our dogs how to live within our expectations and requirements.*

It is unfair to blame our pets for performing normal dog behaviors. Instead, we can design positive ways to change those behaviors. Rather than calling the dog "stupid" or "stubborn" or "spiteful" we need to accept our responsibility in managing the environment and in training the dog to behave in more appropriate and acceptable ways.

Bad Dogs — Getting Rid of Behavior

Many behavior 'problems' result from the dog's natural instincts and behaviors. Often, we are trying to decrease behaviors that are genetically hard-wired into the dog's brain. For example, a Border Collie will naturally chase fast-moving objects. This is a herding behavior that is innate. All of the dog's instincts are pushing it to perform this herding behavior. It can never be completely eliminated, but it can be decreased. If the dog is working sheep, this behavior is necessary and useful. However, if the dog is chasing children or cars, this behavior becomes undesirable and possibly dangerous.

When dealing with genetically-programmed behaviors you have several options. First, you can try to provide an outlet for those instincts. If you own a dog with strong retrieving instincts, and who is always picking up and carrying your possessions, perhaps you can teach him to chase and fetch tennis balls instead. Next, it is important that you monitor the dog very carefully to avoid the behavior at undesired times. For example, do not allow your Jack Russell Terrier to be loose in the front yard if he has a tendency to chase cars.

Simply trying to squash the undesired behavior through punishment will probably be ineffective. The dog will continue to seek out ways to satisfy his urges and desires. Unless you can deliver punishment of just the right

severity, every single time the behavior occurs, and at exactly the right moment, the punishment will probably make the situation worse rather than better. Luckily, there are a number of positive training techniques that will allow us to deal with problem behaviors.

Another problem with simply trying to eliminate undesired behavior is that you cannot have a 'behavioral vacuum'. This means that you cannot remove a behavior and leave an empty space where it once was. The dog needs to do something to fill that space. For example, a dog who rushes the door and jumps on visitors will not be able to passively do nothing at all when visitors enter, even if he has been punished for rushing and jumping. Giving the dog a more appropriate and acceptable alternative behavior to perform can address this issue and will be discussed further.

II. Behavior Modification Techniques

All of the following techniques are based on scientifically tested learning theories. These methods, alone and in combination, can be used to solve a variety of behavior problems. These techniques can work on people as well!

Response Prevention

Every time a dog performs a behavior that is self-reinforcing, the probability of that behavior being repeated increases. If your dog does not have the opportunity to practice the behavior, it is less likely to become a habit. If you leave your dog unattended in the back yard for hours on end, you might think that you are giving him a wonderful chance to enjoy the great outdoors. Your dog may well enjoy his time outside, but he may become bored and start looking for ways to liven up his day. Barking, digging, eating flowers, finding ways to escape, and scratching at the back door are all habits that may result from a lack of supervision and stimulation.

In using response prevention, these unwanted behaviors would not be given the chance to occur. You would simply not leave the dog outside when he was unsupervised. While this is more difficult for the owner, and deprives the dog of some freedom, it effectively limits the dog's chances of developing bad habits. Response prevention allows you to avoid the problem and is one part of a good management plan.

Distraction & Planning

Dogs and puppies behave like human toddlers. They are curious about their environments, love to explore, have no fear, and love putting things in their mouths. Parents of toddlers have learned to cope with these behaviors through the use of distraction. A smart parent will divert his or her child from the electric socket by pointing him in the direction of safer toys and activities. When taking a trip with a toddler, a smart parent is prepared with novel and interesting toys and activities, as well as with adequate snacks. On a long airplane trip I once observed a mother with a child about eighteen months old. She spent time getting the child settled in, gave him some juice during takeoff, regularly got up and took short walks around the cabin with him, provided three or four small snacks, read short stories to him, and offered him different toys before he got bored with the current ones. The child was perfectly quiet and content, and eventually napped for the remainder of the trip. All of the airline passengers appreciated this mother's efforts! She clearly understood the importance of preparation and planning in keeping her child happy and busy. If left to his own devices, the child in the above example would probably have become cranky and bored, would have annoyed other passengers, and could have made everyone miserable for the entire flight.

Dog owners could learn a lot from this mother's example. Rather than leaving things to chance and hoping for the best, she actively planned ways to keep her child engaged and interested. She took his short attention span into account and frequently changed activities. She was proactive in considering ways to deal with the child's possible behavior issues, rather than waiting until trouble occurred and reacting.

Imagine that you have brought home a new puppy and he is very active. He races around the house, grabbing and trying to eat anything he can find. His nickname is probably "Jaws". You could be reactive. You would find yourself chasing him around constantly prying things out of his mouth. You would quickly become annoyed with the puppy and your developing relationship with him would become strained. However, you could avoid most of these problems if you were to take the proactive approach. You would anticipate that your puppy is going to need lots of different activities, and also that he needs to chew on things. You would provide a variety of activities that include walks, new chew toys, short training sessions for treats, supervised free time in the house and yard, and nap time in a confined area. When you see your puppy getting cranky or bored, switch activities. Just like tired toddlers, sometimes hyperactive and irritable puppies simply need some quiet time and a nap. The proactive owner plans for these situations and recognizes them when they occur.

Don't wait for trouble and respond to it. Plan for trouble and avoid it.

Extinction

The term extinction refers to the loss of a behavior. When a behavior is extinguished, it is removed or eliminated. Extinction occurs when a behavior is no longer reinforced. Any behavior that does not have some type of reinforcement will eventually disappear. While this definition and explanation are very simple, carrying out extinction effectively can be a bit more complicated.

First, you need to identify the reinforcers that are maintaining a behavior. What is the payoff? What makes the behavior enjoyable or rewarding? A fundamental law of behavior is that we only continue to do things that have a positive consequence. Sometimes it is very easy to identify the consequence that maintains the behavior. For example, imagine that your dog has the tendency to steal your shoes and chew on them. Chewing is rewarding in and of itself; it's one of those self-reinforcing behaviors. In this case, it is pretty easy to see the positive consequence for your dog. Sometimes, however, identifying the consequence can be a bit more difficult. Imagine that your puppy barks in his crate, even after you yell at him. What is maintaining the behavior? There are several possibilities. First, sometimes barking can be self-reinforcing. Some dogs simply love to hear the sound of their own voices. However, it may be that the yelling is actually reinforcing the behavior rather than punishing it. How could that be the case? It might be that your puppy is desperate not to be alone, and that hearing your voice, no matter what the tone, is reinforcing.

KEY CONCEPT: *We only continue to behave in ways that have a positive consequence.*

Once you have identified the reinforcement for any particular behavior, the next step is to find a way to remove it. When a behavior is self-reinforcing (the pleasant consequence comes simply from performing the behavior) there is no way to remove the reinforcement. Digging, chewing, and chasing squirrels are all examples of self-reinforcing behaviors. Extinction will not work in these cases, but the other behavior modification techniques can be applied successfully.

The other very common consequence that maintains behavior is attention. For some dogs, as with some children, any attention (positive or negative) is reinforcing. In school, the class clown might get in lots of trouble for his behavior, but at least people are paying attention to him, so he continues. For some people, and some animals, being ignored is much worse than being in trouble. When this is the case, our attempts at punishment often have the opposite of their intended effect. If you find yourself in a situation in which a behavior is continuing, or even increasing, despite your efforts to punish it, you may actually be reinforcing the behavior.

The actual process of extinction is a simple one, but requires patience and perseverence. Once the reinforcement for a behavior is removed, the trainer simply ignores the behavior. It will eventually decrease, then disappear. However, this will not necessarily happen in a quick and smooth fashion. Typically, the undesired behavior increases at first. If the dog has been used to receiving reinforcement for his actions, he will probably try harder when that reinforcement doesn't arrive as expected. This is called an extinction burst. I always tell my clients that when they try extinction things will get worse before they get better. If you expect this to occur, then you won't become upset and give up when it happens. Once the extinction burst passes the behavior will begin to decrease. However, even after the behavior seems to have disappeared, it is highly likely that spontaneous recovery will occur. Spontaneous recovery almost always happens during the extinction

At some point, the undesirable behavior comes back in full force...

process. At some point, usually when you think the undesired behavior is gone, it returns in full force. This is another time that trainers consider giving up on this technique and using some other method to try to eliminate the problem behavior. This is where persistence will pay off. Once spontaneous recovery has occurred and passed, true extinction is attained. There is an enormous amount of scientific research the demonstrates the effectiveness of extinction. It truly does work, but you need to be aware of the typical course of progress so you don't give up on it too soon.

Differential Reinforcement of an Alternate Behavior (DRA)

As I stated earlier, we cannot have a behavioral vacuum. If you want to remove or eliminate a behavior, one very effective technique is

DRA. In using DRA, you decide on a more acceptable and appropriate behavior than the one you want to decrease, and heavily reinforce that behavior. You are replacing an undesirable behavior with a desirable one. The best way to approach this technique is to ask yourself "what do I want the dog to do in this situation?", then train that behavior in a positive manner.

While establishing the desired behavior using DRA, you can also use response prevention for the undesired behavior. For example, imagine that I want to teach my dog to chew on his toys (the appropriate behavior) rather than on my shoes (the inappropriate behavior). I would first prevent shoe chewing by being extremely vigilant about where I leave my shoes. Then I would provide my dog with a variety of desirable chew toys at different times. Because chewing is self-reinforcing, I don't really need to add any other reward for chewing on the toys. However, I would probably praise and pet my dog, at first, for choosing the chew toys.

We can use a slightly different twist on differential reinforcement. In differential reinforcement of an incompatible behavior (DRI), we choose and reinforce a behavior that cannot be performed at the same time as the undesired one. Imagine that my dog barks when visitors come into the house. A very appropriate alternate, incompatible behavior might be to pick up and bring the visitor a toy rather than to bark. Since it is difficult to carry a toy in his mouth and bark at the same time, the dog will have to choose the most reinforcing behavior. If I have taught and highly reinforced the dog for bringing toys, he will choose the desired behavior.

Once you understand the concept of differential reinforcement, it can be a very effective technique in a number of situations. It takes an understanding of reinforcement and a bit of creativity, but it is a very useful method for behavior modification.

Negative Punishment

In negative punishment, you are removing something in order to decrease behavior. The thing we take away needs to be something that our subject doesn't want to lose. With children, we often take away a specific toy or the opportunity for a favorite activity. With dogs, we can remove our attention or their freedom. Losing either of these things is unpleasant for most dogs and they are motivated to avoid this type of loss.

It is important that the connection between losing something and the undesired behavior is clear to the dog. This may take a number of repetitions. When using negative punishment, it is vital that the removal of the desired object or activity occur as close as possible in time to the undesired behavior. It is also vital that this connection occur consistently over a number of trials.

One of the behaviors for which negative punishment is very successful is puppy nipping (discussed earlier in the 'Puppy Problems' section). Young puppies don't realize how sharp and painful their nipping can be. Rather than apply a physical punishment (which often makes the problem worse), removing freedom and attention through negative punishment can solve the problem fairly quickly and without any unpleasant side effects. The most important thing about using negative punishment for puppy nipping is that the consequence immediately and consistently follows the behavior. Whenever puppy teeth touch human skin the puppy is put into his crate for a 2-minute time-out. He gets minimal interaction while being put into the crate, and no attention for two minutes. Then he gets out to try again. This procedure must be repeated without emotion as many times as necessary. If this is done properly within several days almost all puppies will stop nipping.

This type of consequence (removal of attention and freedom) is much more pleasant than common techniques that involve hitting, slapping, yelling, etc. These physical corrections may actually cause some puppies to escalate the nipping into more serious biting. Other puppies may become hand-shy and fearful. Neither of these outcomes will lead to a good relationship with your puppy.

To use negative punishment most effectively, you need to identify something that your dog doesn't want to lose. You can then use the removal of that object or activity as an unpleasant consequence for undesired behavior. The contingency (connection) between the action and the removal must occur quickly and regularly. If you can

accomplish this, the negative punishment should work fairly quickly.

Counterconditioning

Counterconditioning is used to teach the dog a new, more appropriate response to a stimulus. The stimulus can be anything, but is often a person, a dog, or some type of activity. The stimulus is often called a trigger as it triggers an automatic response from the dog. If you recall from an earlier chapter in this book, the stimulus-response connection is a type of learning called classical conditioning. There is no conscious thought involved between the exposure to the stimulus and the response. It happens automatically. Some behavior problems occur because the dog responds in an inappropriate way to the stimulus. For example, whenever your dog sees a child run by he begins barking hysterically and tries to chase after him.

To use counterconditioning effectively you must be able to identify the trigger. You must also be very observant so that you can tell when your dog is about to engage in the response. Often, there are subtle warning signs that signal the beginnings of the unwanted response. Many dogs will change their breathing patterns, tense, stare, raise their hackles slightly, etc. Finally, you need to be able to quickly intervene BEFORE the unwanted behavior occurs. When you intervene, you want to find some way to change your dog's response to the stimulus. As you can imagine, the use of this technique requires good observational skills and quick responses on the part of the trainer. However, counterconditioning works very well when dealing with behaviors that are automatic responses to stimuli.

The easiest way to change a dog's automatic response is to get him to focus on something else and to relax slightly. Most of the responses we want to change are based on over-excitement and arousal. If we can find a way to induce the dog to be calmer and more relaxed, we can avoid the response. To induce this calmer emotional state, food is commonly used. The dog cannot eat and be overly excited at the same time. The process of eating in itself focuses and calms the dog. When using food for counterconditioning, choose something small, soft, and very, very desirable to the dog. The key is to catch the dog once he has noticed the stimulus, but before he has begun the full-blown response, and to present him with the food. Timing is crucial for the success of this process. If you wait too long to offer the food, the dog will be too excited and will be unable to eat. You want to be sure that the dog has noticed the stimulus, but hasn't yet begun the response.

The food is then given in small bits in a constant, steady stream. As long as the dog is able to eat, he should be fed the treats. Once the stimulus is no longer present, stop feeding. For best effect, counterconditioning should be combined with systematic desensitization (described next).

Systematic Desensitization

Systematic desensitization is a planned, step-by-step program for gradually exposing the dog to a stimulus (trigger). The purpose of systematic desensitization is to slowly and carefully raise the dog's level of exposure to the stimulus, while keeping his response at a minimum. In people, this technique is often used and is very successful in dealing with fears and phobias. Systematic desensitization works because of a learning process called habituation. Habituation refers to a decrease in response with continued exposure to a stimulus. With habituation, we get used to the presence of a stimulus and then eventually we ignore it. I experienced this process myself years ago when radar detectors in cars were popular. At first, I responded appropriately by slowing down whenever I heard the radar detector sound. After some time being exposed to the sound of the radar detector (and not seeing a police car in sight) I began to respond less and less, then eventually not at all. Of course, eventually I did get a speeding ticket while ignoring the sound of the radar detector. The police officer actually laughed as he approached my car and heard the radar detector still sounding!

While the process of habituation did not work in my favor in that particular instance, we can use it to help our dogs learn to ignore certain stimuli. The key is to start exposure to the stimulus at a very low, barely noticeable level. While the stimulus is present, we induce relaxation by continuously feeding the dog. Once the dog is able to ignore the stimulus at a given level, we make the stimulus slightly more noticeable and continue the process. By proceeding in this slow, gradual manner, we can actually make progress relatively quickly.

Here is an example of how you might use counterconditioning and systematic desensitization in the case of a dog who tries to chase after running children. I would use this technique in the case where a dog actually likes children, but their running triggers a chase response. Before you begin, keep in mind that it is your responsibility to keep others safe around your dog. Even a small dog could knock down, frighten, and hurt a child, so proceed with due caution. If you have any doubts about your ability to physically restrain and control your dog, consult a professional trainer.

When working on a problem like this, I would have the dog in a head halter. You could also use a well-fitting martingale collar. Be absolutely sure that your dog will not be able to slip out of his collar during this process. Use a strong 6 foot leash made of either leather or nylon. You want to keep the leash loose (between your hand and the dog's head) during this process, but be sure that it will stop the dog's movement forward if necessary.

You then need to have access to and control of the stimulus. If you have older children who will carefully follow your directions, they can be very helpful in your training. Start out with the child standing still at a distance. Your dog should notice the child, but not react. Feed the dog continuously for a minute or so then have the child leave the dog's sight and stop feeding the dog. Wait about 30 seconds, then have the child return and take a few steps back and forth while you feed the dog. Then have the child leave and stop feeding. Have the child return and jump up and down in place while you feed the dog. Then have the child leave and stop feeding. Have the child return and slowly jog a few steps back and forth while you feed the dog. Then have the child leave and stop feeding. This process all takes place with the child at a distance. Once the dog does not respond at all to the child at a distance, the steps are repeated with the child slightly closer.

This technique is described very clearly by Jean Donaldson in her excellent book 'The Culture Clash'. She calls it 'bar is open/bar is closed'. When the stimulus is present the 'bar is open' and the dog is continuously fed. When the stimulus leaves the 'bar is closed' and there are no more treats. The constant feeding in the presence of the trigger leads the dog to form a different response to the sight of the trigger. Instead of "run and chase" the dog learns "wait for the goodies to come my way". This is a much safer and more appropriate response.

If the dog ignores the treats and attempts to engage in the undesired response, you will need to move back and present the trigger at an easier level (more distance, less movement, etc.) If you move ahead too quickly, your dog may regress and perform the automatic response. If this happens it is telling you that the stimulus is too compelling to the dog and you need to make it easier for your dog to succeed.

Analyzing Behavior Problems

When faced with a canine behavior problem, most dog owners have no idea how to begin solving the problem. When we face difficulties with our dogs, it can be very upsetting and emotional. If we respond in an emotional manner, things will probably only get worse. We need to be calm, objective, and organized in our approach to solving problems. It helps to have a structured way to consider the problem and its possible solutions. One way to consider and analyze behavior problems is presented in this section.

Question #1 (the behavior): What is the dog doing?

This question focuses only on overt, observable behaviors. Don't get into considering the 'why' of the behavior yet. Just list what you see the dog doing. Be as clear and specific as possible. Saying "my dog is aggressive" is neither clear nor specific. The term 'aggressive' can mean very different things. Break it down into the actions that you can observe. For example, saying that "my dog growls and snarls when people approach my door" is a much better descriptor of behavior. Clients often tell me "my dog is out of control". I then question them about what the dog is actually doing. 'Out of control' might mean jumping on guests in excitement or it might mean

nipping and biting children. Before a problem can be solved, it has to be clearly identified.

KEY CONCEPT: When analyzing behavior problems, focus on the specific actions that the dog is performing.

Question #2 (the consequences): What happens after the dog performs the undesired behavior?

Identifying consequences is vital to determining what maintains the behavior. Consider both immediate and delayed consequences. How does the dog's behavior change the environment? What do you do after the dog performs the behavior? What do other people involved do? Again, be clear and specific. There may be a variety of consequences for any particular behavior. For example, if your dog is growling and snarling when the mail carrier approaches your house, several things may occur. You might grab your dog and yell at him (sometimes). Your child might try to calm the dog by holding him by the collar and stroking him. Your husband might throw a toy or offer a treat in order to distract the dog. The mail carrier will probably continue to deliver the mail, then leave. After the mail carrier leaves your dog may pace around the living room for a few minutes before laying down.

Once you identify all the possible consequences, it is easier to see why the behavior continues. Some, and possibly all, of the consequences must be reinforcing to the dog.

Question #3 (the antecedents): What happens immediately before the undesired behavior?

What factors lead to the occurrence of the behavior? Does it only happen when someone walks up to your front door? Does it only occur at a certain time of day or in a specific situation? Who is present immediately before the behavior begins? There are usually specific triggers that your dog is responding to that lead to the behavior. You need to identify those triggers.

An example analysis:

When you take your dog for a walk he behaves aggressively when he sees other dogs.

1. What is the dog doing?
The term 'aggressive' is a useless descriptor. You might note that the dog strains at the end of the leash, barks in a high-pitched tone, and spins in circles.

2. What happens after the dog performs the undesired behavior?
Do you talk to your dog, drag him away, try to calm him by petting him, grab him by the collar and yell at him? What do the other dogs and people do? Do they cross the street? Do they stop? Do they turn and walk away?

3. What happens immediately before the undesired behavior?
Does your dog stiffen and growl when he sees a dog approaching from a distance? Do you tighten your grip on the leash? Do you talk to your dog? Does the other dog make eye contact with your

dog or vocalize? Does the other person say anything?

Generating solutions:

Once you have answered these three questions as clearly and completely as possible, you can begin to consider solutions for your dog's problem behavior. There are usually a number of ways to design possible solutions. You may need to experiment with several in order to find the one that works best in any given situation. Before you actually do anything, sit down and consider these questions.

1. Can you avoid the triggers or change your dog's response to them?

2. Can you remove the reinforcement that is maintaining the behavior?

3. Can you train an alternate behavior?

For the above example you might generate some of the following ideas:

1. Can you avoid the triggers or change your dog's response to them?

You could avoid the triggers by avoiding taking walks with your dog. This would work, but it wouldn't solve the problem and it would deprive both you and your dog of exercise.

You could attempt to change your dog's response to the triggers by using counterconditioning and systematic desensitization.

2. Can you remove the reinforcement that is maintaining the behavior?

What are the reinforcing consequences in this situation? Are your reactions somehow contributing to the way your dog reacts? Could your attempts at calming your dog actually be taken as praise and reinforcement?

Is the fact that the other dog leaves a reward to your dog? Could he be trying to keep the other dog at a distance?

3. Can you train an alternate behavior ?
What would you like your dog to do instead? Can you choose a more appropriate behavior and train that? Instead of lunging, barking, and spinning you could start reinforcing your dog for staying at your side or for looking at you.

Aggression

Aggression refers to behaviors that are designed to harm others. Aggression has many causes and can take many forms. It is difficult to impossible for an untrained pet owner to deal with aggression in a safe and effective manner. Traditional trainers often use force and punishment in an attempt to decrease or eliminate aggressive behaviors. Typically, these techniques cause more problems than they solve. The use of force leads to an increase in aggression in many dogs. Also, while some traditional techniques will seem to work short-term, in the long-term the problem becomes worse.

Aggression problems do not get better on their own. Typically, they escalate over time and become worse without effective treatment. It is vital that you contact a qualified trainer or behaviorist if your dog is behaving in ways that concern you. You are ethically and legally responsible for your dog's behavior. Manage the situation so that your dog does not have the opportunity to harm anyone, and seek help immediately.

KEY CONCEPTS REVISITED:

We only continue to behave in ways that have a positive consequence. If there is no reinforcement, a behavior will eventually decrease, then disappear. If your dog is continuing to perform a behavior, it is rewarding to him in some way. One way to eliminate the behavior is to remove the reinforcement.

When analyzing behavior problems, focus on the specific actions that the dog is performing. Describe only what you actually see. Your interpretation of what is happening, and your explanation for why it is happening, may lead you in the wrong direction. In behavioral psychology we are interested in the observable behaviors.

Further reading:
Clicker Fun: Click & Fix (video) *by Deborah Jones, Ph.D.*
Toolbox for Remodeling Problem Dogs *by Terry Ryan*
Clinical Behavioral Medicine for Small Animals *by Karen Overall, M.A., V.M.D., Ph.D.*

Chapter 8

Training as a Lifestyle

— *Time + Training = Success* —

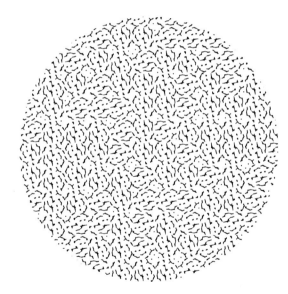

I. Finding Time to Train

The biggest problem most people have with training their dogs is simply finding the time to do it. Most of us are already feeling stretched to the limit with our responsibilities, and adding another time-consuming task seems impossible. Years ago, when I took my first obedience class, the instructor told us to train for an hour a day. I dutifully worked for an entire hour at one stretch each day. While my dog did learn the exercises, we both also learned that training could be quite a chore. It's hard to be fun and exciting for an entire hour every single day. The enjoyment we both found in training diminished quite quickly. In addition, carving out that hour's worth of time in a single block was often very difficult.

Luckily, it's not necessary, or even desirable, to train for an hour at a time in order to achieve success. In fact, the best way to train is in a number of much shorter sessions spread throughout the day. The shorter sessions allow the dog to concentrate on one or two exercises at a time, rather than trying to intergrate a wide variety of information. They also allow you to stop training while the dog is still enthusiastic and interested. Working for too long can cause fatigue and a lack of excitement about training. Because we want our dogs to enjoy training and to have a positive attitude about it, shorter but more frequent training sessions are ideal.

Depending on the dog, training sessions of between 2 and 10 minutes are best. Young puppies and dogs who have short attention spans and are easily distracted need the shortest training sessions. The old adage 'leave them wanting more' applies well to dog training. Hard as it might be, it is much better to stop before your dog wants to. Developing your dog's positive attitude towards training is a crucial element to success. If you overtrain, your dog will 'burn out' and lose enthusiasm. No matter how good the training technique, it will not work well unless the dog is a willing partner in the process.

So, when do you have a couple of extra minutes in your day? Can you allow an extra five minutes in your morning routine? What about a few minutes during commercials when you're watching a television show? Just before you feed your dog is an ideal training time. Could you take a few minutes before each meal? A quick training session in the middle of your dog's evening walk would be easy to add. There are plenty of opportunities available if you are only looking to carve out a few minutes at a time. Take advantage of them and you will be amazed at the results.

II. Preparing for Success

In terms of making the learning experience as effective as possible, a large amount of research suggests that shorter, more frequent training sessions will result in faster learning and better recall. Training for the same amount of time will be much more effective if the time is broken into small blocks, rather than one large one. If you have 30 minutes for training,

using that time in 3 sessions of 10 minutes each or 6 sessions of 5 minutes each will be a much better strategy than using the time all at once. Remember cramming for exams? This technique typically does not result in long-term retention of information. It is also unduly tiring and stressful. In psychology we refer to this phenomenon as massed vs. spaced practice. Spaced practice is always a better choice.

KEY CONCEPT: *Short, frequent training sessions are best.*

Most formal training classes, by necessity, run for about an hour once a week. During an hour class you (and your dog) may learn and practice a large number of exercises. Clearly, this is not an optimal learning experience for either humans or dogs, but it is usually more practical. If you take classes you can approach class time as an introduction to the material and a chance to observe, experiment with techniques, and ask questions. Neither you nor your dog are likely to actually learn the behaviors within that hour. Real learning takes place with repetition during your practice sessions between classes.

In your training sessions, focusing on only one or two exercises will be the most effective way to help your dog learn. This allows your dog to concentrate completely on each exercise and to process that information. Trying to practice many different exercises in an individual session may lead to incomplete learning and confusion.

Be ready to train when the opportunity arises. Your main training tools are a clicker and treats. If you have to search through the kitchen drawers for your clicker, then spend 5 minutes collecting treats, you will be wasting precious training time. If you are not ready when your training opportunity presents itself, you will probably not even bother. However, if you have clickers and treats within easy reach, you are more likely to take advantage of those possible training moments when the occur. I can probably put my hands on a clicker and treats within 30 seconds. I always have my training bag packed and in my car. I have a clicker on the kitchen counter and one on my dresser in the bedroom. Most of my coat pockets contain a clicker and a plastic bag with a few treats. By having my training tools readily accessible, it greatly increases the likelihood that I will actually train my dog when I can carve out a few free moments.

Being successful in training also requires having a plan. A training plan can be fairly general or it can be quite detailed and specific. However, without any plan, you won't make a lot of progress. You need to know what your short-term and long-term training goals are. Then, you need to think about what it will require to reach those goals. Short-term goals are those you are looking for on a daily and weekly basis. Long-term goals can be monthly and beyond. Your training plan is your road map for getting to your ultimate training goals. It can really help to keep a small notebook or training log, and simply jot down what you've done for each session. You will probably be surprised, when you look back over your training book, at how quickly you and your dog have progressed. It's nice to be able to chart your progress in black and white.

KEY CONCEPT: *Being successful in training requires having a plan.*

For example, let's say that you are working on the 'down'. For the first two days, you plan on moving from luring the down with food to fading out the lure and using it only every 5th or 6th time. Then, for the next two days, you plan on increasing the criteria and asking for the down (still luring randomly) in a number of different places (in the bathroom, in the garage, while you're on walks, on the front porch, etc.) Then, for the next two days, you plan on completely fading the lure and adding the verbal cue right before the behavior. Finally, you will continue to ask for the down in increasingly distracting settings. At the end of a week or so, you should find that your dog's response to the 'down' cue is becoming very reliable.

You may have loftier, more ambitious goals. For example, you may want to train your dog to pass a therapy dog certification test so that he can visit hospitals and nursing homes. First, find out what the actual requirements of the certification test will be. Look at each of the final required behaviors as a goal. Then break down the steps that will be necessary to teach each behavior. In the Delta Society certification test, your dog must sit quietly at your side while someone approaches you and shakes your hand. The steps start with teaching a sit at your side, then increasing the duration of the sit, then adding the distraction of a person approaching and talking to you. Over several weeks of planned practice, your dog can learn to perform this behavior.

Goals are achieved in very, very tiny steps. In order to succeed you need an understanding of where you eventually want to be, and of how to break down your goals into very small increments. While changes in your dog's behavior from one training session to the other may be barely perceptible, continued work will lead to major changes over time. Don't discount the importance of a 2 or 3 minute training session, it can lead to great changes.

III. Couch Training

By nature, I am a very lazy human being. I don't like to work hard. My idea of bliss is a day when I have absolutely no responsibilities. Because of my basic slothful nature, I have designed training techniques that require very little time and energy. Even if you are a much more energetic and ambitious person than I am, there are sure to be times when you don't have much time or desire to train. That's when 'couch training' can come in very handy. As the name implies, these exercises can all be trained while you stay off your feet. I say, let the dog do the hard work!

One way to carve out some training time is to do 'commercial training'. When you are watching television have your clicker, treats, and a favorite toy handy. Whenever commercials come on, train the dog. You certainly won't be missing much! Actually, you will discover that commecials take up more airtime than you ever imagined. You'll get plenty of training in. When the program comes back on tell the dog he's 'free' and go back to watching the show. If you are reading you could plan a 2-3 minute training break at the end of each chapter. It will also give you a chance to rest your eyes, clear your mind, and stretch your muscles.

Some of my favorite 'couch training' exercises follow:

Recalls —
It's easy to practice 'treat toss' recalls while you laze on the sofa. Simply show your dog a treat and encourage him to chase it when you toss it behind him. Then, once he eats that treat call him back to you. Click and treat when he comes. Repeat, throwing the treat further and in different directions.

You can also practice having different family members call the dog back to them once the treat is tossed. Everyone should have a clicker and treats. The dog must return to the correct person to get his reinforcer.

Distance sits & downs —
To begin, toss a treat behind your dog and encourage him to chase it. Once he eats the treat give him either a 'sit' or 'down' cue. When he responds, click and toss another treat behind him. Repeat the process. At first, your dog may return to you before he sits or lies down. That's fine. Go ahead and click, tossing the treat behind your dog so he has to

go away from you to get it. Over time, your dog will discover that it is more efficient for him to sit or down where he is when he hears the cue, because the treat will be tossed behind him, rather than coming from you.

When your dog starts responding quickly at a distance you can alternate sit and down cues. You can also practice using just a verbal cue or just a hand signal. You can also practice having your dog hold the sit or down for varying amounts of time before you click and toss the treat.

Go out (run away) —
You might wonder why it would be desirable to teach your dog to run away from you. Most people work very hard at teaching the dog to come to them! However, teaching your dog to go away from you can be a fun and useful behavior. In agility and obedience competitions your dog needs to learn this behavior as a basis for advanced training.

I teach this behavior with a favorite toy. Show the dog the toy and throw it behind him, clicking as he turns to chase it. Repeat, adding a verbal cue (go, run away, scram, etc.) just before you throw the toy. As your dog starts to anticipate the thrown toy he will respond to the verbal cue and turn to run away before you throw it. Be sure to click this behavior and follow immediately by throwing the toy.

You can combine the 'go out' with a sit or down at a distance. Once your dog will run away from you on cue, ask for a sit or down, then click and reinforce.

It's easy to practice treat toss recalls while you laze on the sofa...

Back-up —
This exercise also involves having your dog move away from you, but in this case he is moving backwards. To begin training this exercise, hold a treat or toy that your dog really wants. Then simply wait. He will probably try out a number of behaviors, but you're waiting for any slight movement backwards. Watch his feet. When he makes even the smallest move away from you backwards, even just adjusting his weight backwards, click and reinforce by tossing the toy or treat over his head and behind him.

Most dogs can learn to back-up fairly easily. As your dog starts to understand what you want, increase the number of backwards steps he must take before you reinforce him.

Retrieve —
Most dogs love to chase after a thrown toy. The problem can be getting them to bring it back to you. One way to encourage your dog

to return to you with the toy is to offer a double incentive for doing so. Practice retrieves using two identical toys. Throw one for your dog, encourage him to return by showing him the other. In addition, when he does return offer him a treat as well. This makes it worth his while to bring the toy back.

If your dog wants to play keep away with the toy he has ignore him. Play with the toy you have instead. Toss it in the air and catch it. Make it sound like you're having a great time. Ignore your dog until he returns close to you. If there is another person around, play catch with him or her using the second toy. Make it clear that the dog doesn't get to join in unless he is willing to play by your rules. He has to bring the first toy back to you before he gets to play with the second one.

Many dogs can spend hours playing fetch in the living room. This is a great way to give your dog exercise during bad weather or when you are tired. Also, if your dog is healthy and doesn't have any structural problems (bad knees, hips, etc.) you can encourage him to play fetch up and down the stairs. Toss a toy down the steps, let him chase it, then encourage him to bring it back up to you. This will wear most dogs out fairly quickly.

Spin (both ways) —
You can teach your dog to spin by luring him in a circle with a treat. Click and give him the treat after the spin. Fade the lure and continue using a circling hand motion as a cue. Add a verbal cue before the hand motion. To avoid confusing your dog, teach the spin in one direction only at first. Once that behavior is well-learned, add a spin in the opposite direction. Most dogs naturally have a preferred turning direction, go with that one first. Over time you can fade the hand motion to a smaller hand signal.

My three dogs can do synchronized spinning. All three respond to the same spin cue at the same time. When I was training this, I would only reinforce the dogs who responded correctly to the cue. If a dog missed the cue or was slow, he/she did not get a treat. They quickly learned to do this together as a group.

Dead dog —
Everyone loves a good 'bang! you're dead' performance. A 'dead dog' goes down on his side or on his back and lies perfectly still once the cue is given. You can use either shaping or luring to get your dog to move into the desired position. Then you will want to add duration, so your dog will remain still until released. You can add a cute cue such as a shooting motion and a verbal 'bang!'.

This behavior can be taught with your dog at your feet while you sit on the sofa.

Stop & go —
Stop & go is actually a slow recall combined with a stand stay. The goal is to have your dog approach you, then stop and wait at your cue, then come forward again, then stop and wait, etc. Think of it as a red light / green light game. You call the dog forward, then stop him and ask him to wait, then call him again, stop him again, etc. Start teaching this

behavior by calling your dog to you, then asking him to wait. Your dog is likely to at least hesitate, this is when you should click and treat. Then call again and ask for another wait, etc.

Speak —

Most dogs have the ability to make a number of different vocalizations. If you are really worried about turning your dog into a barker, then don't try this. However, it is usually the case that once you put barking on cue, your dog is less likely to offer it when the cue is not present.

One way to get your dog to make noise is to find a way to get him excited or frustrated. I do this by playing with the dog until he's very excited, then holding his toy and encouraging him to bark. When he makes any noise at al I click and throw the toy for him. With Katie, my Lab, I taught her to speak by holding her dinner bowl and waiting for her to make any sound at all. Then I'd click and give her a piece of her kibble.

I.V. Training Activities

If you really get bitten by the dog training bug, there are a number of organized dog sports and activities that you can participate in. Most people who pursue dog training as a hobby or profession started out by taking a basic obedience class for an unruly or unmanageable pet. Many professional trainers discovered that they had a fascination with the training process and that they wanted to understand more about the way that dogs learn.

If you enjoy participating in organized activities with your dog, a little bit of research will lead you to others with the same interests. Most areas have an American Kennel Club (AKC) affiliated club that offers training classes. Most AKC affiliated training clubs focus on training for conformation (the show ring) and competition obedience. Many are also starting to offer agility training. There are usually also a number of private trainers and schools in any given geographic area. Check out all of the possibilities and try to find a place where the people and the dogs look like they're having fun while they're learning.

Conformation

Dogs who are shown in conformation are judged on their physical appearance and structure. Purebred dogs of any given breed are compared to the breed standard. In theory, the dog who conforms most closely to the ideal standard for the breed is chosen as the winner on that given day. Conformation dogs must be kept intact (not spayed or neutered) while being shown as this competition is considered an evaluation of possible breeding stock. There are different classes for male and female dogs, and for dogs of different ages. In some breeds dogs may be separated by coat type or by color.

In the conformation ring dogs are presented before the judge. They must be physically examined (including teeth and genitals!) and they must demonstrate how well they move. Conformation dogs must be trained to tolerate all sorts of handling, to gait (move at the proper speed on a leash), and to stack (stand quietly while being observed and examined). In addition, they must learn to tolerate the sometimes noisy and crowded dog show environment without becoming overly stressed or anxious.

All of the required behaviors for conformation can be clicker trained starting at a very early age. Many conformation competitors currently use the clicker only as an attention-getting device. While this will certainly work, they have yet to realize the actual value of clicker training specific behaviors.

Canine Good Citizen

The American Kennel Club developed the Canine Good Citizen (CGC) program as a way for all dogs to demonstrate a basic level of acceptable behavior, training and control. Dogs are tested on their responses to a series of simple temperament and obedience tests on a pass/fail basis. The dog must pass each of the ten tests in order to earn the CGC designation.

The tests:
1. *Accepting a Friendly Stranger.*
An evaluator approaches you while your dog holds a sit stay by your side. The evaluator will greet you and shake your hand.

2. *Sitting Politely for Petting.*
An evaluator approaches your dog while he is in a sit stay at your side, greets you, and pets your dog.

3. *Appearance and Grooming.*
An evaluator lightly brushes or combs and also pets and gently handles your dog.

4. *Out for a Walk.*
You will walk your dog on a loose lead. You will make turns and halt when directed.

5. *Walking Through a Crowd.*
You will walk your dog on a loose lead through a crowd. The crowd may consist of 3 or more people who are all moving about.

6. *Sit and Down on Command / Staying in Place*
You will ask your dog to sit, and then to lie down. The dog will be asked to stay while you walk about 20 feet away, then return to him.

7. *Coming When Called.*
You will ask your dog to either sit or down and stay, walk about 20 feet away, and call him to you.

8. *Reaction to Another Dog.*
An evaluator with a dog will approach you and your dog. You and the evaluator will shake hands.

9. *Reaction to Distractions.*
The evaluator will test your dog's response to distractions. The distraction might be a noise (dropping a book, pan, or chair behind your dog). The distraction might also be movement (a person jogging in front of your dog or

pushing a shopping cart or riding a bicycle).

10. *Supervised Separation.*
You hand your leash to a helper and leave your dog with him or her as you go out of sight for 3 minutes.

To obtain a passing score on each of the tests, your dog must remain calm and must respond reasonably well to your cues and signals. In the CGC you are allowed to give multiple cues and signals, and to praise your dog as appropriate. You are not allowed to have food or toys during the testing. A dog who passes the CGC test has demonstrated that he will behave well in most reasonable public situations.

Competition Obedience

In obedience competitions, dogs are trained to perform a set of specific exercises and are judged on how well those exercises are performed. There are three basic difficulty levels: Novice, Open, Utility. At each level, the dog must pass the minimum requirements three times, each time showing under a different judge. The dog is then awarded the title for that level.

The exercises in the Novice level consist of walking a specified heeling pattern with the handler. The dog must heel on the handler's left side, close to her leg. The pattern consists of turns, halts, and changes of pace (fast and slow). The judge calls out the directions as the dog and handler perform the pattern. The dog needs to move with the handler and

A dog who passes the CGC has demonstrated that he will behave well in most reasonable public situations…

respond to the handler's movements. The dog will perform the heeling pattern first on-lead, then later off-lead. A Figure Eight exercise is also performed on-lead. The dog and handler circle around two people standing about eight feet apart. Again, the judge directs the dog and handler through the pattern. The Stand for Exam is another Novice exercise. The dog must stand at the handler's signal, then stay while the handler walks six feet away. The judge then approaches the dog, who should remain still, and lightly touches the dog on the head, shoulders, and back. The handler the returns around the dog and releases him. In the Recall exercise the handler leaves the dog on a sit stay and walks across the ring. The handler then turns to face the dog and, when the judge directs, calls the dog to her. The dog must come directly to the handler and sit in front of her. The handler will then be directed to have the dog 'finish' or move to her left side and sit. Finally, a group of dogs will perform the Long Sit and Long Down together. Dogs are lined up and are directed to sit. Handlers must leave their dogs and walk across the ring, then turn to face the line of dogs. After one minute the handlers are instructed to return. They return by walking past the sitting dogs, going around behind them, and ending with their dogs on their left sides. The down is done in the same way, but the dogs must hold their positions for three minutes. For someone who is new to training these exercises may sound impossibly difficult, but they are actually attainable for almost all dogs. After passing Novice three times the dog receives the right to be called a Companion Dog (CD). The dog is then eligible to compete at the Open level in obedience.

In Open the dog and handler will again perform an off-lead heeling pattern. They will also perform the Figure Eight exercise off-lead. The Drop on Recall consists of the handler leaving the dog on sit stay, crossing the ring, and turning to face the dog. When the judge directs, the handler calls the dog. Somewhere in the middle of the recall the judge will direct the handler to give the dog a down cue or signal. The dog is expected to respond promptly and to lie down. The judge then directs the handler to call the dog again. The dog is expected to complete the recall and sit in front of the handler until signaled to finish. There are two retrieve exercises in the Open level. In the Retrieve on Flat the dog sits and waits at the handler's side while she throws a dumbbell at least eight feet away. When the judge directs, the handler sends her dog to fetch the dumbbell. The dog should respond promptly, should go directly to the dumbbell and pick it up, and should bring it directly back to the handler, sitting in front and holding the dumbbell until the judge directs the handler to take it and to finish the dog. The Retrieve Over High Jump has the same basic requirements, but the handler tosses the dumbbell over a solid jump. The dog must go out over the jump to retrieve and must also take the jump on the way back to the handler. In the Broad Jump exercise the dog is left on a sit stay in front of a flat, wide jump. The handler stands next to the jump and, on the judge's signal, directs the dog to take the jump. The dog is then expected to jump and to return and sit in front of the handler, who has made a quarter turn while the dog was in the air. The dog is then directed to finish. The Long Sit and the Long Down are made harder at this level by adding more duration (3 minutes for the sit and 5 minutes for the down) and by adding the requirement that the handlers must completely leave the area while the dogs perform the exercises (out of sight stays). While the exercises in Open are definitely challenging and require hard work and effort, they can also be enjoyable and interesting. After passing Open three times the dog earns the right to be called a Companion Dog Excellent (CDX). The dog is then eligible to compete in Utility.

In Utility the heeling pattern is combined with a series of exercises that the dog must perform on hand signal only (signal exercise). The handler may not use any verbal cues during heeling or during the position changes that are required. The heeling pattern is also more complex at this level. At the end of the heeling pattern the judge directs the handler to 'stand your dog', then to 'leave your dog'. The handler must then move to the other end of the ring and turn to face the dog. The judge will direct the handler to have her dog lie down, then sit, then perform a recall, then a finish. All must be done with hand signals only. The dog is expected to respond promptly to each signal. The Scent Discrimination exercise is a very interesting requirement for this level. The handler provides a set of scent articles (leather and metal dumbbells). The set of articles is scattered on the floor in a basic circular pattern. The handler puts her scent one of the articles by rubbing it with her hands. The scented article is put into the pile on the floor while the dog and handler face the opposite direction. The dog and handler turn to face the pile and the handler directs the dog to find the scented article. The dog must use his nose to search for the correct article, then pick it up and return to sit in front of his handler, holding the correct article until the judge directs the handler to take the article and then to finish her dog. This exercise is performed twice in a row, once with a leather scented article and once with

a metal scented article. In the Directed Retrieve three identical cloth gloves are placed in a row across one end of the ring. The dog and handler face the opposite direction and the judge tells the handler which glove the dog is expected to retrieve. The dog and handler then turn to face the glove and the handler gives a cue and signal for the dog to retrieve. The dog must retrieve the correct glove and return to front position, holding the glove until the handler takes it and directs the dog to finish. In the Moving Stand for Exam exercise the handler and dog are directed to start heeling in a straight line. When the judge says 'stand your dog' the handler directs the dog to stay and continues on about ten feet across the ring alone. The judge then approaches the dog and examines him by touching his head, running his hands over the dogs shoulders, down the legs, down the back, over the hips, and sometimes even over the tail. The dog is expected to remain perfectly still during the examination. The judge then directs the handler to call the dog to heel position (rather than coming in front the dog must go directly to the handler's left side). Finally, the Directed Jumping exercise is performed. Two jumps are set, one at each side, halfway across the ring. The handler and dog stand at one end of the ring, facing the two jumps and centered halfway between them. On the judge's signal the handler sends her dog to run straight away from her, between the jumps, to the opposite side of the ring. The handler then cues the dog to turn and sit facing her. The handler must then direct the dog (both cue and signal) to take one jump or the other (the judge decides which will be first). The dog should take the indicated jump, return to sit in front, then finish on cue. The exercise is then repeated, directing the dog to take the other jump. When you and your dog complete the entire Utility routine three times your dog has earned the right to the title of Utility Dog (UD). This is quite an accomplishment!

Each and every one of the requirements for competition obedience can be successfully trained using the clicker and positive reinforcement. Breaking the exercises down into their smallest parts and teaching them slowly and systematically will lead to a dog who understands the exercises and who is confident in performing them. Clicker training is quite new to many obedience competitors. Traditional training techniques are still quite common. However, as competition obedience trainers gain a better understanding of the power of this method, and as they see the results that clicker trained dogs can achieve, it will definitely gain more acceptance and popularity.

Agility

Agility is probably one of the fastest growing and most popular dog sports in the United States. Agility is fast, fun, and exciting, both for dogs and handlers. Think of it as a giant, timed obstacle course for your dog. Your job is to train your dog to safely and successfully perform the obstacles, and to listen to your direction. While agility requires a solid foundation of obedience training and control,

it is less rigid and structured than obedience competition.

Agility courses typically include the following obstacles: jumps (including spread jumps), tunnels (open and closed—often called a chute), contact obstacles (A-frame, dog walk, see-saw), a pause table, and weave poles.

Jumps can have single, double, or triple bars. The double and triple bars add distance as well as height to the jump. A long, low broad jump may also be used. A dog's jump height is calculated based on his height at the top of his shoulders.

Open tunnels, sometimes called pipe tunnels can be twisted into different shapes. They can be left straight or twisted into a C or an S curve. Most dogs learn to love tunnels once they experience them. A closed tunnel or chute consists of a barrel shaped opening that has fabric attached. The dog must go through the opening, then push through the fabric to exit the chute. Dogs must be introduced to the chute fabric slowly and carefully so that they do not become frightened or get tangled or twisted in it.

Contact obstacles all involve the dog approaching and climbing the obstacle. Contact obstacles have contact zones on the lower third of the beginning and end of each obstacle. Dogs must always touch the contact at the end (down contact). In some agility organizations, they must also touch the up contact of certain obstacles as well. The A-frame is the widest contact obstacle. In competitions the height is set at a minimum of 5'6" and a maximum of 6'3"in certain organizations. The dog must perform the A-frame by running up one side, over the top, and down the other side. The dog walk is similar to a balance beam, but has an ascending and descending ramp for the dog. The dog must run up the ascending ramp, across the length of the dog walk, and down the descending ramp. The see-saw is the only contact obstacle that moves. The dog begins to climb up the board and, as the dog reaches the middle of the plank, his weight causes the board to pivot so that it descends. The dog is expected to continue on and exit the board as it hits the ground.

The pause table is large enough for the dog to sit or lie down on (the position is chosen by the judge before the competition begins). The height of the table is set appropriately for the height of the dog. The dog must jump up onto the table, assume the required position, and hold that position while the judge completes a count of five.

Weave poles are a series of upright posts that are set at an equal specified distance apart. The dog must enter the weaves poles with the first pole next to his left shoulder. He must then weave in and out through the entire line of poles without missing any. There are between six and twelve poles in a line.

The first task in agility is to teach the dog to perform each of the individual obstacles safely. Requirements for the ultimate performance of each obstacle must be broken down into easily achieved goals. Requirements are raised slowly as the dog becomes comfortable and confident about performing the obstacles. Next, the dog must learn to perform the obstacles in a continuous sequence. Obstacles are first chained together in simple two obstacle sequences such as jump then tunnel. As those are performed successfully longer sequences and more complicated chains can be practiced.

Good agility trainers also teach directional cues signals to help them guide their dogs. For example, the dog would be taught to move closer and to move further away laterally. The dog might also be taught to 'go on' and move out ahead of the handler to perform an obstacle. Cues and signals for upcoming turns are also very helpful in agility.

Agility competitions contain three basic levels of difficulty. In AKC these are called Novice, Open, and Excellent. All three levels contain the same basic obstacles (without weave poles in Novice), but the time allotted to complete the course, the number of obstacles on the course, and the level of difficulty vary. Certain agility organization also offer specialty classes and games such as Jumpers, Gamblers, and Snooker.

The goal of agility is to direct the dog through the course in the proper order of obstacles (determined by the judge), performing each obstacle correctly, and in the fastest time possible. You must earn three qualifying scores at each level to move up to the next level.

Agility can be very enjoyable, both for handlers

and for their dogs. Dogs seem to enjoy performing the skills they have learned. They get to use their natural inclination to run, jump, and climb in a constructive way. Handlers enjoy the strategy involved in planning their agility runs to the dog's best advantage. Most agility trainers are aware of the importance of making training and showing a very positive experience for their dogs. Harsh or unpleasant agility training will typically result in a poor performance. Clicker training is very, very popular in agility because of this. Clickers, treats and toys can be used in teaching and to motivate the dog to perform as well as possible. Many of the very top competitors in agility are clicker trainers.

Pet Therapy

Pet therapy is actually a misleading term. It literally sounds as if the pets are either giving or receiving therapy. The proper term would actually be 'animal-assisted activities'. This refers to using an animal to provide emotional support, distraction, and/or entertainment for those who are ill or confined. This has become a popular, and much needed, activity. A number of groups exist whose members train their dogs for this purpose, and then participate in regular visits to hospitals, nursing homes, hospice patients, etc.

To participate in this type of activity, the dog must have a steady, sound temperament. He must enjoy being petted and handled and spending time with people. He must also remain calm and relaxed, even in very chaotic or stressful situations. He must adapt quickly and well to change. Dogs are born with these temperamental tendencies. While training can produce a dog who is under control and responds to cues and signals, the dog's temperament comes through in stressful situations. A dog may be fine normally, but if he reacts with a growl when startled or snaps when handled roughly, he would not be an appropriate dog for this activity.

In addition to a great temperament, a dog in an animal-assisted activities program must be under complete control at all times. The dog must respond quickly and correctly to all cues and signals. A dog who hesitates when told to come may end up getting run over by a patient in a wheelchair! A dog who does not sit as directed may end up knocking a frail patient off her feet. A dog who wiggles around and won't hold a stay when on a patient's bed may disturb necessary equipment such as IV lines.

There are two major organizations (Delta Society and Therapy Dog International), and a number of smaller ones, who provide testing and certification for dogs who participate in animal assisted activities. The tests are very similar to that for a Canine Good Citizen, with added expectations and requirements that are appropriate to therapeutic settings, such as a dropped bedpan and a person on crutches or in a wheelchair. It is important to earn certification and to have affiliation with a recognized group. They can provide help and assistance in getting started as well as insurance coverage (a definite necessity!)

and a chance for more active involvement with others who have the same interests.

In addition to passing the certification requirements for one of the organizations, it will be both fun and useful to teach your dog tricks to perform during your visits. While a solid sit stay is necessary, others are most impressed by a dog who can roll over or shake hands. Also, dogs who are willing to play 'dress up' and wear costumes are seen as more appealing and friendlier. One of the groups that I visited with at a Children's Hospital required that all the dogs wear t-shirts with the hospital logo (scarves were provided as well). The t-shirts identified the dogs as belonging to the group and also kept the shedding during visits to a minimum. Katie was a big hit with one little girl when she let herself be dressed up in a doctor's surgical cap and mask. People are often apprehensive with large black dogs, so the dressing-up really helped put people at ease around her.

A good Therapy Dog must enjoy being petted and handled and spending time with people…

Other Activities

There are a wide variety of other activities out there as well. Flyball, herding, field trials, frisbee, and tracking can all be taught and titles can be earned if desired. Less formal activities such as backpacking and hiking are gaining in popularity. Some groups meet on a regular basis to take nature walks or to go on short sightseeing trips with their dogs.

Because there are so many activities you can share with your dog, you are certain to find something that fits your interests and that your dog will enjoy. Take into account the time that you have to devote to a dog-related activity, as well as your dog's physical condition and temperament. Dogs love to do things with their people, and a clicker trained dog can be an enjoyable, well-behaved companion.

KEY CONCEPTS REVISITED:

Short, frequent training sessions are best. Both people and dogs learn best when the practice sessions occur more often, but for less time in any one session. Sessions that run between 2 and 10 minutes are ideal. It also helps to focus on one or two new exercises at a time. Introducing a large number of new exercises at once will be confusing for your dog.

Being successful in training requires having a plan. As the old saying goes 'if you don't know where you want to go, you won't know when you get there.' Short-term (daily and weekly) and long-term (monthly and beyond) goals are a good way to organize yourself and to measure your progress. Keeping track of your progress may help motivate you to continue your training.

Further reading:
Train Your Dog the Lazy Way *by Andrea Arden*
Clicker Fun *by Deborah Jones, Ph.D.*
Clicker Training for Obedience *by Morgan Spector*
Canine Adventures: Fun Things to do With Your Dog *by Cynthia Miller*